IN 25 VOLUMES
Each title on a specific drug or drug-related problem

ALCOHOL

Alcohol *And Alcoholism*
Alcohol *Customs & Rituals*
Alcohol *Teenage Drinking*

HALLUCINOGENS

Flowering Plants *Magic in Bloom*
LSD *Visions or Nightmares*
Marijuana *Its Effects on Mind & Body*
Mushrooms *Psychedelic Fungi*
PCP *The Dangerous Angel*

NARCOTICS

Heroin *The Street Narcotic*
Methadone *Treatment for Addiction*
Prescription Narcotics *The Addictive Painkillers*

NON-PRESCRIPTION DRUGS

Over-the-Counter Drugs *Harmless or Hazardous?*

SEDATIVE HYPNOTICS

Barbiturates *Sleeping Potion or Intoxicant?*
Inhalants *The Toxic Fumes*
Quaaludes *The Quest for Oblivion*
Valium *The Tranquil Trap*

STIMULANTS

Amphetamines *Danger in the Fast Lane*
Caffeine *The Most Popular Stimulant*
Cocaine *A New Epidemic*
Nicotine *An Old-Fashioned Addiction*

UNDERSTANDING DRUGS

The Addictive Personality
Escape from Anxiety and Stress
Getting Help *Treatments for Drug Abuse*
Treating Mental Illness
Teenage Depression

TREATING MENTAL ILLNESS

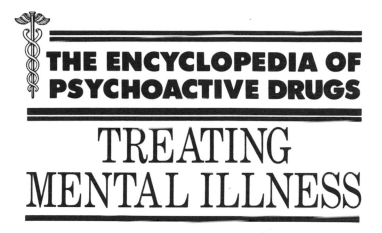

THE ENCYCLOPEDIA OF PSYCHOACTIVE DRUGS

TREATING MENTAL ILLNESS

ROBERT BYCK, M.D.

Yale University School of Medicine

1986
CHELSEA HOUSE PUBLISHERS
NEW YORK
NEW HAVEN   PHILADELPHIA

SENIOR EDITOR: William P. Hansen
PROJECT EDITOR: Jane Larkin Crain
ASSISTANT EDITOR: Paula Edelson
EDITORIAL COORDINATOR: Karyn Gullen Browne
EDITORIAL STAFF: Jeff Freiert
               Perry Scott King
               Kathleen McDermott
               Alma Rodriguez-Sokol
CAPTIONS: Harold Steinberg
ART DIRECTOR: Susan Lusk
ART COORDINATOR: Carol McDougall
LAYOUT: Noreen M. Lamb
ART ASSISTANT: Victoria Tomaselli
PICTURE RESEARCH: Elizabeth Terhune
               Andrea Bonasera
COVER: *Secrets* by Devis Grebu

First printing

Library of Congress Cataloging in Publication Data
Byck, Robert.
     Treating mental illness.

     (The Encyclopedia of psychoactive drugs)
     Bibliography: p.
     Includes index.
     Summary: Discusses mood modifying drugs used to
correct chemical imbalances in the brain which are
believed to cause mental illnesses such as depression
and schizophrenia.
     1. Mental illness—Chemotherapy—Juvenile
literature.   2. Psychotropic drugs—Juvenile literature.
[1. Mental illness.   2. Psychotropic drugs] I. Title.
II. Series.
RC482.B93   1986   616.89'18   85-32564
ISBN 0-87754-774-2

Chelsea House Publishers

133 Christopher Street, New York, NY 10014

345 Whitney Avenue, New Haven, CT 05510

5014 West Chester Pike, Edgemont, PA 19028

CONTENTS

Foreword 9

Introduction 13

1 An Overview 19

2 Antipsychotic Drugs 37

3 Depression 53

4 Manic-Depressive Psychosis 65

5 The Future 73

Appendix 1: Symptoms of Clinical Depression 74

Appendix 2: Symptoms of Mania 75

Appendix 3: Symptoms of Schizophrenia 76

Appendix 4: State Agencies 78

Further Reading 84

Glossary 85

Index 91

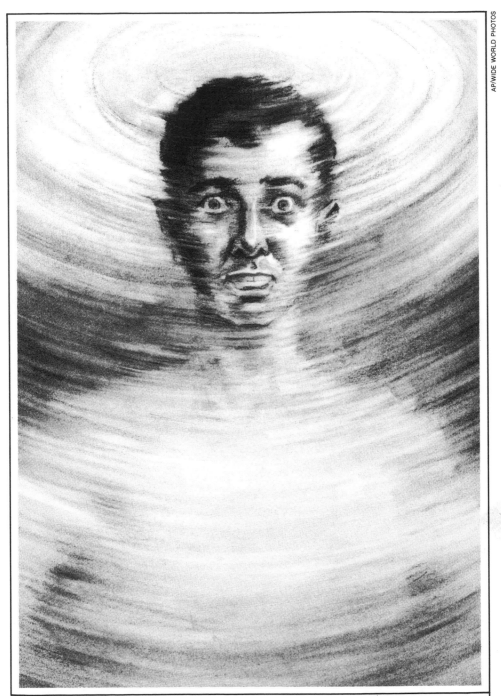

This drawing dramatically captures the feelings of dreadful anxiety and frantic confusion that beset many mental patients as they try to survive in a world that they do not understand.

8

FOREWORD

In the Mainstream of American Life

The rapid growth of drug use and abuse is one of the most dramatic changes in the fabric of American society in the last 20 years. The United States has the highest level of psychoactive drug use of any industrialized society. It is 10 to 30 times greater than it was 20 years ago.

According to a recent Gallup poll, young people consider drugs the leading problem that they face. One of the legacies of the social upheaval of the 1960s is that psychoactive drugs have become part of the mainstream of American life. Schools, homes, and communities cannot be "drug proofed." There is a demand for drugs—and the supply is plentiful. Social norms have changed and drugs are not only available—they are everywhere.

Almost all drug use begins in the preteen and teenage years. These years are few in the total life cycle, but critical in the maturation process. During these years adolescents face the difficult tasks of discovering their identity, clarifying their sexual roles, asserting their independence, learning to cope with authority, and searching for goals that will give their lives meaning. During this intense period of growth, conflict is inevitable and the temptation to use drugs is great. Drugs are readily available, adolescents are curious and vulnerable, there is peer pressure to experiment, and there is the temptation to escape from conflicts.

No matter what their age or socioeconomic status, no group is immune to the allure and effects of psychoactive drugs. The U.S. Surgeon General's report, "Healthy People," indicates that 30% of all deaths in the United States

Patients and employees of a psychiatric hospital in Oregon pull a log from the Grand Ronde River during a camping trip. This outing was part of an experiment exploring new ways of treating the mentally ill.

are premature because of alcohol and tobacco use. However, the most shocking development in this report is that mortality in the age group between 15 and 24 has increased since 1960 despite the fact that death rates for all other age groups have declined in the 20th century. Accidents, suicides, and homicides are the leading cause of death in young people 15 to 24 years of age. In many cases the deaths are directly related to drug use.

THE ENCYCLOPEDIA OF PSYCHOACTIVE DRUGS answers the questions that young people are likely to ask about drugs, as well as those they might not think to ask, but should. Topics include: what it means to be intoxicated; how drugs affect mood; why people take drugs; who takes them; when they take them; and how much they take. They will learn what happens to a drug when it enters the body. They will learn what it means to get "hooked" and how it happens. They will learn how drugs affect their driving, their schoolwork, and those around them—their peers, their family, their friends, and their employers. They will learn what the signs are that indicate that a friend or a family member may have a drug problem and to identify four stages leading from drug use to drug abuse. Myths about drugs are dispelled.

National surveys indicate that students are eager for information about drugs and that they respond to it. Students not only need information about drugs—they want information. How they get it often proves crucial. Providing young people with accurate knowledge about drugs is one of the most critical aspects.

THE ENCYCLOPEDIA OF PSYCHOACTIVE DRUGS synthesizes the wealth of new information in this field and demystifies this complex and important subject. Each volume in the series is written by an expert in the field. Handsomely illustrated, this multi-volume series is geared for teenage readers. Young people will read these books, share them, talk about them, and make more informed decisions because of them.

Miriam Cohen, Ph.D.
Contributing Editor

Extraction de la Pierre de Folie *by Hieronymus Bosch shows a "surgeon" removing the "stone of madness" from a patient's head. Throughout history societies have invented remedies, some successful, some not, for insanity.*

INTRODUCTION

The Gift of Wizardry
Use and Abuse

JACK H. MENDELSON, M.D.

NANCY K. MELLO, PH.D.

Alcohol and Drug Abuse Research Center
Harvard Medical School—McLean Hospital

Dorothy to the Wizard:

"I think you are a very bad man," said Dorothy.
"Oh, no, my dear; I'm really a very good man; but I'm a very bad Wizard."

—from THE WIZARD OF OZ

Man is endowed with the gift of wizardry, a talent for discovery and invention. The discovery and invention of substances that change the way we feel and behave are among man's special accomplishments, and like so many other products of our wizardry, these substances have the capacity to harm as well as to help. The substance itself is neutral, an intricate molecular structure. Yet, "too much" can be sickening, even deadly. It is man who decides how each substance is used, and it is man's beliefs and perceptions that give this neutral substance the attributes to heal or destroy.

Consider alcohol—available to all and yet regarded with intense ambivalence from biblical times to the present day. The use of alcoholic beverages dates back to our earliest ancestors. Alcohol use and misuse became associated with the worship of gods and demons. One of the most powerful Greek gods was Dionysus, lord of fruitfulness and god of wine. The Romans adopted Dionysus but changed his name to Bacchus. Festivals and holidays associated with Bacchus celebrated the harvest and the origins of life. Time has blurred the images of the Bacchanalian festival, but the theme of drunkenness as a major part of celebration has survived the pagan gods and remains a familiar part of modern society.

13

The term "Bacchanalian festival" conveys a more appealing image than "drunken orgy" or "pot party," but whatever the label, some of the celebrants will inevitably start up the "high" escalator to the next plateau. Once there, the de-escalation is difficult for many.

According to reliable estimates, one out of every ten Americans develops a serious alcohol-related problem sometime in his or her lifetime. In addition, automobile accidents caused by drunken drivers claim the lives of tens of thousands every year. Many of the victims are gifted young people, just starting out in adult life. Hospital emergency rooms abound with patients seeking help for alcohol-related injuries.

Who is to blame? Can we blame the many manufacturers who produce such an amazing variety of alcoholic beverages? Should we blame the educators who fail to explain the perils of intoxication, or so exaggerate the dangers of drinking that no one could possibly believe them? Are friends to blame— those peers who urge others to "drink more and faster," or the macho types who stress the importance of being able to "hold your liquor"? Casting blame, however, is hardly constructive, and pointing the finger is a fruitless way to deal with problems. Alcoholism and drug abuse have few culprits but many victims. Accountability begins with each of us, every time we choose to use or to misuse an intoxicating substance.

It is ironic that some of man's earliest medicines, derived from natural plant products, are used today to poison and to intoxicate. Relief from pain and suffering is one of society's many continuing goals. Over 3,000 years ago, the Therapeutic Papyrus of Thebes, one of our earliest written records, gave instructions for the use of opium in the treatment of pain. Opium, in the form of its major derivative, morphine, remains one of the most powerful drugs we have for pain relief. But opium, morphine, and similar compounds, such as heroin, have also been used by many to induce changes in mood and feeling. Another example of man's misuse of a natural substance is the coca leaf, which for centuries was used by the Indians of Peru to reduce fatigue and hunger. Its modern derivative, cocaine, has important medical use as a local anesthetic. Unfortunately, its increasing abuse in the 1980s has reached epidemic proportions.

The purpose of this series is to provide information about the nature and behavioral effects of alcohol and drugs, and the probable consequences of their use. The information presented here (and in other books in this series) is based on many clinical and laboratory studies and observations by people from diverse walks of life.

Over the centuries, novelists, poets, and dramatists have provided us with many insights into the beneficial and problematic aspects of alcohol and drug use. Physicians, lawyers, biologists, psychologists, and social scientists have contributed to a better understanding of the causes and consequences of using these substances. The authors in this series have attempted to gather and condense all the latest information about drug use and abuse. They have also described the sometimes wide gaps in our knowledge and have suggested some new ways to answer many difficult questions.

One such question, for example, is how do alcohol and drug problems get started? And what is the best way to treat them when they do? Not too many years ago, alcoholics and drug abusers were regarded as evil, immoral, or both. It is now recognized that these persons suffer from very complicated diseases involving complex biological, psychological, and social problems. To understand how the disease begins and progresses, it is necessary to understand the nature of the substance, the behavior and genetic makeup of the afflicted person, and the characteristics of the society or culture in which he lives.

The diagram below shows the interaction of these three factors. The arrows indicate that the substance not only affects the user personally, but the society as well. Society influences attitudes towards the substance, which in turn affect its availability. The substance's impact upon the society may support or discourage the use and abuse of that substance.

Although many of the social environments we live in are very similar, some of the most subtle differences can strongly influence our thinking and behavior. Where we live, go to school and work, whom we discuss things with—all influence our opinions about drug use and misuse. Yet we also share certain commonly accepted beliefs that outweigh any differences in our attitudes. The authors in this series have tried to identify and discuss the central, most crucial issues concerning drug use and misuse.

Regrettably, man's wizardry in developing new substances in medical therapeutics has not always been paralleled by intelligent usage. Although we do know a great deal about the effects of alcohol and drugs, we have yet to learn how to impart that knowledge, especially to young adults.

Does it matter? What harm does it do to smoke a little pot or have a few beers? What is it like to be intoxicated? How long does it last? Will it make me feel really fine? Will it make me sick? What are the risks? These are but a few of the questions answered in this series, which, hopefully, will enable the reader to make wise decisions concerning the crucial issue of drugs.

Information sensibly acted upon can go a long way towards helping everyone develop his or her best self. As one keen and sensitive observer, Dr. Lewis Thomas, has said,

> There is nothing at all absurd about the human condition. We matter. It seems to me a good guess, hazarded by a good many people who have thought about it, that we may be engaged in the formation of something like a mind for the life of this planet. If this is so, we are still at the most primitive stage, still fumbling with language and thinking, but infinitely capacitated for the future. Looked at this way, it is remarkable that we've come as far as we have in so short a period, really no time at all as geologists measure time. We are the newest, the youngest, and the brightest thing around.

A 17th-century engraving of moonstruck (lunatic) women dancing in the street. Insanity has inspired fear throughout the ages. Only in the 20th century have we begun to deal with mental illness in an enlightened way.

A collage entitled Minds In Torment *serves to illustrate the state of a person suffering from mental illness. Many emotional disorders are physiologically based and can be treated by prescribed psychiatric drugs.*

CHAPTER 1

AN OVERVIEW

Research into the chemistry of the brain has revealed the physiological basis of many types of mental illness. With this knowledge scientists have been able to develop specific drugs to treat a wide range of emotional disturbances. Although many of these drugs are powerful and mood altering, they rarely produce any therapeutic effect on so-called "normal" people. Furthermore, unlike illegal drugs, psychiatric drugs are rarely if ever abused. This book will discuss these drugs, focusing on how they work, when they are beneficial, and the type of patients for whom they provide help.

Mental Health Professionals

Mental disorders are treated by a number of different kinds of professionals. Although only medical doctors can prescribe and administer psychiatric drugs, a brief description of the various types of people who work with the mentally disturbed will provide a helpful overall picture of the mental health field.

A *psychotherapist* is an individual trained to use one of the many forms of "talking therapy" that have been developed from various theories on how to treat psychological disorders. Rather than using drugs to treat mental disorders, a psychotherapist relies on discussion techniques that help patients examine their feelings about themselves and their lives. A psychotherapist may also have various other professional qualifications, such as a graduate degree in social work.

A *psychiatrist* is a medical doctor (M.D.) who has also taken four years of training in the treatment of mental disease. Psychiatrists are trained to distinguish between the symptoms of physical disease and the symptoms associated with psychological disorders. Their training usually enables them to practice individual, family, and group psychotherapy. Because they are physicians, they can legally prescribe drugs.

Sigmund Freud, the father of psychoanalysis. According to Freudian theory, mental illness is often caused by a person's attempt to repress painful past experiences.

THE BETTMANN ARCHIVE

A *psychoanalyst* is a professional trained and certified to practice psychoanalysis, a method used to reveal to patients psychological conflicts that they are unaware of. Usually, but not always, the psychoanalyst is a physician trained in psychiatry. Psychoanalysis is a form of treatment developed from the theories of the Austrian psychiatrist Sigmund Freud (1856–1939). Psychoanalysts believe that mental illness often is caused by the repression of painful past experiences. They feel that by bringing forgotten memories to the surface, the sources of psychological conflicts can be located. If the patients are made aware of these conflicts, the psychological disorders can be diminished or eliminated.

This type of therapy may involve treatment four or five times a week. During these sessions the psychoanalyst employs specific and clearly defined techniques that help patients recall forgotten and repressed experiences and relate them to their current behavior. Although psychoanalysts rarely prescribe drugs, they are legally entitled to do so if they are also physicians.

A *psychologist* is a person who usually has an advanced degree, often a Ph.D., in clinical psychology. He or she practices many kinds of psychotherapy, including behavior therapy, a technique that uses rewards and punishments to change the way people act. Many psychologists are well trained in the diagnosis of mental illness. Few, however, are experienced in recognizing the differences between physical illness and mental disease. Because they do not have medical degrees they are not allowed to prescribe drugs.

Historical Background of Psychiatric Drugs

In the middle of the 19th century the French physician J. J. Moreau de Tours noted the remarkable similarity between some of the symptoms associated with mental disease and the psychological state caused by the use of hashish, a drug made from the *Cannabis sativa* plant. His book *Hashish and Mental Illness* was one of the first works to suggest that mental disorders might be caused by chemical imbalances in the body rather than by environmental or psychological factors. More than a century later scientists are still debating the extent and importance of these biochemical (the chemical reactions in living organisms) factors. Many researchers now believe that the root causes of most mental disturbances are associated with chemical changes in the central nervous system (the system in the body that includes the brain and spinal cord and that coordinates physical activity). Whatever the cause may be, one fact is now certain. It is possible to reduce the symptoms of many psychiatric illnesses with drugs that affect the central nervous system.

Many of the drugs now being used in the treatment of mental disorders were first developed in the 1950s. Modern *psychopharmacology*, or the study of the effects of drugs on the mind, is frequently traced to Albert Hofmann's discovery of LSD in the late 1940s. Nevertheless, the notion that *mental* illness is similar to *medical* illness can be traced to the 19th century, when some scientists proposed anatomical and chemical imbalances as the cause of mental disorders.

A revolution in the treatment of mental illness occurred in the early 1950s. Henri Laborit, a French neurosurgeon (a physician who treats disorders of the central nervous system), was researching ways to prevent complications that occurred after surgery. He combined antihistaminic drugs (drugs that oppose the action of histamines, chemicals found in all body tissues and particularly associated with inflammation and allergic reactions) with other drugs given to patients prior to surgery. One of these antihistamines, promethazine, produced a state described as "euphoric quietude," a calm feeling of well-being.

In 1951 a new drug, 4560 RP, also known as chlorpromazine, was sent to Laborit, who experimented with the drug as a preventative against surgical shock and as a way to speed up anesthesia. Laborit noticed that 4560 RP produced sleepiness and what he called "disinterestedness" (lack of interest in the environment) in patients. Although some psychiatrists had used 4560 RP in combination with other drugs in sleep therapy, Laborit was the first doctor to describe the drug's unique effects in reducing anxiety and agitation. He encouraged psychiatrists to administer it to patients.

Unlike all previous forms of treatment for psychosis, chlorpromazine seemed to have a long-term, dramatic effect on many different types of mental disorders. Its discovery ushered in a new era in psychiatry. News about the success of this revolutionary drug in treating mental illness spread quickly, and within five years it was being widely prescribed in French mental hospitals. Researchers reported that the drug was most effective in reducing the symptoms of psychosis when administered continuously for several weeks. Scientists began synthesizing and testing other similar compounds, until a wide range of drugs soon existed for the treatment of psychosis.

In 1949 an Australian psychiatrist, John Cade, discovered lithium, a new drug that successfully treated the manic stage of manic-depressive psychosis. (This disease is characterized by abrupt alternations of depression and mania, or frantic elation.) However, it would be almost 20 years before lithium was accepted into psychiatric practice.

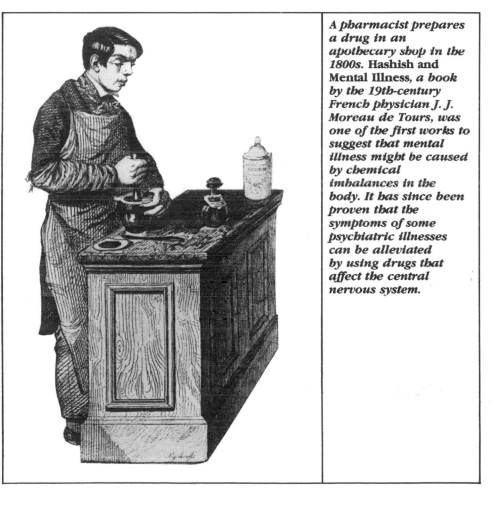

A pharmacist prepares a drug in an apothecary shop in the 1800s. Hashish and Mental Illness, *a book by the 19th-century French physician J. J. Moreau de Tours, was one of the first works to suggest that mental illness might be caused by chemical imbalances in the body. It has since been proven that the symptoms of some psychiatric illnesses can be alleviated by using drugs that affect the central nervous system.*

In India in the 1950s another breakthrough occurred —
the discovery of a drug called *reserpine*. This drug was extracted from the root of *Rauwolfia serpentina*, or snakeroot,
a plant that had been used as a folk remedy for insanity for
hundreds of years. The term *tranquilizer* was first used to
describe the calming and mood stabilizing effects of reserpine, which was used to treat psychosis.

Drugs for Mental Illness

Pharmacologists and doctors divide drugs into three cate-
gories. Over-the-counter drugs, the most familiar, are usually
readily available to the general public at pharmacies, super-

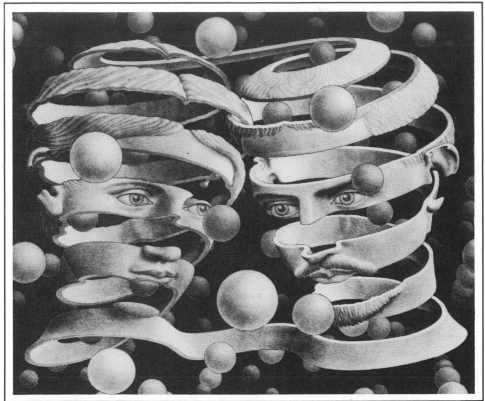

ART RESOURCE

Bond of Union, *a painting by the well-known Dutch contemporary artist*
Maurits Cornelis Escher, articulates the complex relationship between
patient and therapist. Two of the basic requirements for successful
psychoanalytic treatment are honesty and trust.

markets, and grocery stores. Prescription drugs can be obtained only with a doctor's prescription. And lastly, there is a varied group of drugs that are used in self-treatment. They are often dangerous and sometimes illegal.

Over-the-counter drugs, or OTCs, include a large group of preparations of varying effectiveness. They include such medicines as ointments, cough medicines, and aspirin. Once they have been tested and approved by the Food and Drug Administration (FDA), OTCs are considered safe enough to be taken in the recommended doses without the advice of a doctor. OTCs are of no use in the treatment of psychiatric illnesses.

Prescription drugs are available only with a doctor's prescription. Possession of these drugs by anyone other than the person for whom the prescription was written is technically illegal. Prescription drugs are usually quite safe if used as directed. However, if the wrong dosage is taken or the wrong drug is prescribed for a particular illness, these drugs are potentially very dangerous.

Certain prescription drugs fall under the 1970 Controlled Substances Act, and are "scheduled," meaning it is likely they may be abused. For example, heroin is a Schedule I drug (the category that includes the most dangerous drugs) because it has no accepted medical use and has a high potential for abuse. Amphetamine is a Schedule II drug, which means that it has some accepted medical use and some potential for abuse. Though all of the drugs discussed in this volume are prescription drugs, none of them are scheduled. This means that the drugs used for the treatment of psychiatric illnesses neither lead to addiction nor produce pleasurable effects in "normal" individuals.

Self medication often includes the use of drugs to regulate mood. These drugs may be commonly available substances, such as nicotine, alcohol, and caffeine, or illegal drugs such as heroin, marijuana, and cocaine. People often use drugs to try to treat the symptoms of their mental illness. Those who suffer from depression or anxiety may, for example, take sleeping pills or *antianxiety* (tension reducing) drugs. Others turn to heroin, cocaine, or amphetamines, in the mistaken belief that these illegal drugs can relieve their depression. In fact, "self-medication" is often the beginning of serious drug abuse problems. Such substances may be not only addictive but also physically and psychologically destructive. The long-term use of these drugs can only lead the user into serious drug abuse, thus compounding the very problems the sufferer was trying to treat.

Drug Names

Like all prescription drugs, each *psychotherapeutic* (a drug used for treating psychiatric illness) has several names. For example, 2,chlorophenothiazine is the chemical name of the drug more commonly referred to in medical usage by its generic name, chlorpromazine. In addition, drug manufacturers give their products trade names. In France chlorprom-

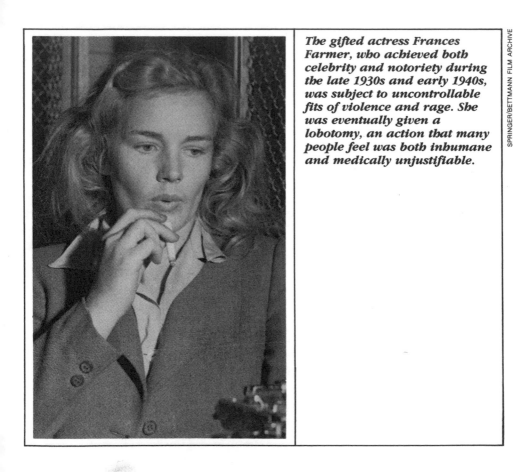

The gifted actress Frances Farmer, who achieved both celebrity and notoriety during the late 1930s and early 1940s, was subject to uncontrollable fits of violence and rage. She was eventually given a lobotomy, an action that many people feel was both inhumane and medically unjustifiable.

SPRINGER/BETTMANN FILM ARCHIVE

azine was given the trade name Largactil. When it was introduced into the United States, the American drug manufacturer chose the trade name Thorazine. Today chlorpromazine has many other trade names, including Chloramead and Promapar.

Drugs are also given group names, which indicate their effects or therapeutic purposes. For example, chlorpromazine and other similar drugs were categorized in France as neuroleptic drugs. Today they are often called *antipsychotic drugs*, a term more descriptive of the use to which they are put. In this book we will discuss *antipsychotic drugs* (medications used to relieve mental disturbances), as well as *antidepressant drugs* (medications used to relieve depression) and *mood-stabilizing drugs*. These terms, although useful, are not necessarily fully descriptive. We can also refer to many

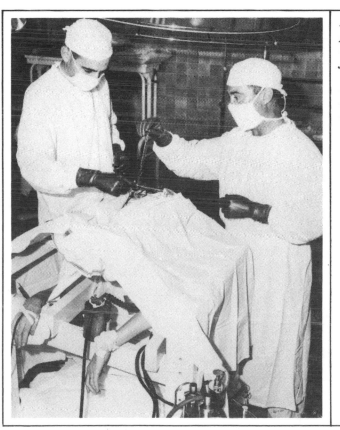

AP/WIDE WORLD PHOTOS

Neurosurgeons perform a pre-frontal lobotomy, which is a form of brain surgery used by some doctors to treat people suffering from violent and seemingly incurable forms of psychosis.

of the antipsychotic drugs as *antihistaminic drugs*, thereby describing them according to their pharmacological action rather than by their therapeutic purpose. This class could also be called *dopamine-blocking drugs*. Here we are using as a descriptive term a specific effect that those drugs have on *dopamine* (a neurotransmitter, or a chemical present in the body that conveys signals between nerves).

Another way to name drugs is by their chemical group. For example, chlorpromazine is a *phenothiazine*, the name of the basic chemical that was modified to synthesize chlorpromazine. Drugs can also be classified by their chemical structure. One group of antidepressants is called *tricyclic*

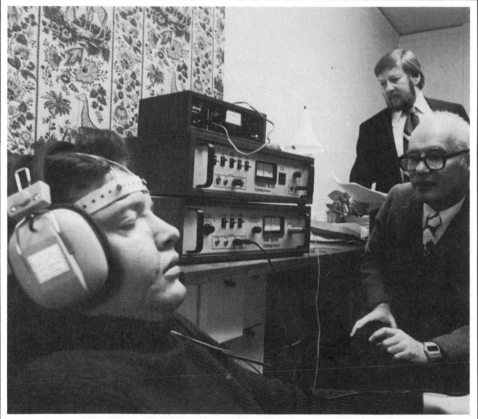

Scientists study sleep patterns of a patient they have taught to doze off naturally, without the aid of sleeping pills. Sleep therapy for psychiatric illness had its origins in the mid-19th century.

antidepressants, because the drugs in this particular group have three rings of carbon atoms in each molecule.

Drugs and Their Effects

Psychopharmacology, a specialized area within the field of pharmacology, is the study of the origin, properties, and effects of drugs that alter emotions and behavior. Scientists working in the area of pharmacology have discovered some general principles that hold true for all drugs. Before we examine the drugs used to treat mental illness we need briefly to review these principles.

A tablet press used in the production of aspirin. Like the psychotherapeutic drugs, aspirin does not cure a disease, but rather decreases or alleviates the symptoms.

The specific chemical reactions produced by drugs in the body are quite complicated and irrelevant to our discussion. However, knowing the structure of a drug that has therapeutic, or beneficial, effects can serve as a guide for chemists who hope to synthesize a new drug with similar actions. Unfortunately, most new drugs have been discovered accidentally.

One general principle of pharmacology is that the dose of a drug is directly related to the drug's effects. The higher the dose, the greater the effects. Unfortunately, this also holds true for side effects (undesirable effects of the drug). The effectiveness of a treatment is therefore frequently limited by the side effects that may occur. However, sensitivity to the various effects of any given drug differs from patient to patient. One person may react to a particular drug with such

The aftereffects of a heroin dose. Heroin, which is a physically addictive and highly dangerous narcotic, is sometimes seen as a last resort by individuals seeking an escape from their problems through mindless oblivion.

severe trembling or shaking that use of the drug must be discontinued. Somebody else may be better able to tolerate the symptoms. When prescribing a drug, a doctor must take into account not only the type of drug and its potency, but also the individual patient.

For a drug to be effective in treating mental illness it must affect the brain, where the disturbance is located. Most psychotherapeutic drugs, however, also affect other organs besides the brain. It is frequently those effects that are noticed first by the patient. Patients taking psychotherapeutic drugs must have an open relationship with their doctor so that they can feel free to discuss any suspicions or anxieties about side effects. The doctor may, for example, be able to adjust the dosage or the drug-taking schedule so that the patient suffers less from the side effects. Some of these undesirable side effects can be treated with other drugs.

Most of us are familiar with the effects of alcohol and aspirin. We can learn a few things about all drugs by thinking about the characteristics of alcohol and aspirin and how they relate to psychotherapeutic drugs. Alcohol is a drug that acts on the brain and changes the functioning of mental processes. Because it is quickly absorbed through the stomach into the blood, we feel alcohol's effects quickly. Some of the side effects, such as nausea and stomach irritation, can be local (confined to a specific part of the body). Once the alcohol is absorbed, we begin to experience the mental effects, while the liver starts to detoxify the alcohol, or chemically change it to an inactive substance that is excreted, or eliminated, by the kidneys. Although all drugs go through the same processes of being absorbed and excreted by the body, not all drugs are detoxified. Some are still for the most part unchanged when they are excreted by the kidneys.

Unlike alcohol, most psychotherapeutic drugs stay in the body for a long period of time. Because they have what is known as a long duration of action, psychotherapeutic drugs can be taken in the evening and continue to have beneficial effects throughout the next day. As with alcohol and most other drugs, the effects of psychotherapeutic drugs will intensify and sometimes change as the dosage is increased.

Aspirin, like the psychotherapeutic drugs, cannot cure a disease, but rather decreases or removes the symptoms. Taken in recommended doses by a healthy person, aspirin will have no obvious effect on the brain. Most psychotherapeutic drugs, however, do affect "normal" people, but the immediate effects of these drugs are usually their side effects, not the desired effects. The higher the dose, the stronger the effect. Many of these drugs cause sleepiness and interfere with activities that require concentration, such as driving.

As we mentioned earlier, people have different levels of tolerance for the side effects of psychotherapeutic drugs. Some of these side effects can be lessened by the use of other drugs, but others are an apparently necessary cost of treatment. Drug treatment of psychiatric illness is a powerful and radical approach, and it should be used only when the possible benefits outweigh the possible risks.

Treating Mental Illness

The symptoms of mental illness may appear gradually and go unnoticed for some time. However, a person who has trouble functioning or maintaining personal relationships should certainly seek — or be encouraged to seek — professional help.

Someone who experiences a sudden onset of symptoms of mental illness should be seen immediately by a doctor. Such symptoms may be the result of drug use, of physical illness, or of a physical change in the brain, such as a tumor. Once the doctor has determined that the problem is a psychiatric illness — one related to disorders of thought, behavior, and mood — the use of psychotherapeutic drugs in treating the disease may be considered. The severity and duration of the symptoms usually determine whether the disturbance is best treated with drugs. Many people who have become distressed with the events or patterns in their lives may require psychotherapy to work out the problems. Depending on the severity of the patient's symptoms, a doctor may recommend both psychotherapy and drugs.

Nancy: A Case Study

Nancy was a troubled 17-year-old high school student who, over the previous six months, had become secretive and isolated, frequently locking herself in her room. She took no interest in her physical appearance, and her performance at school deteriorated sharply. She constantly heard voices that she felt were controlling her life, telling her she was a bad person who should be punished. To calm herself, she began to smoke marijuana. Nancy had become decidedly paranoid, afraid that her family and friends were trying to harm her. Plagued by morbid fantasies about food and a fear that dead animals would poison her, Nancy refused to eat meat. She often used nonsensical words to express her thoughts.

When asked by a doctor to describe her feelings, Nancy said with no emotion: "I am dead, and you are all rotting. Rottingham is meat. That's the place where we can meet."

A scene from the movie The Snake Pit, *which portrayed the horrible conditions of an American insane asylum of the 1940s. This film focused national attention on the need for improving conditions in psychiatric wards.*

Further investigation uncovered a history of mental illness in Nancy's family. Her paternal uncle, who suffered from recurrent nervous breakdowns, had been in and out of mental hospitals for years. Most significantly, it also became clear that the deterioration of Nancy's mental health began just after the sudden death of her father in a car accident.

A psychiatrist dealing with someone like Nancy must consider a number of possibilities. Perhaps her bizarre behavior and anxieties were induced by the abuse of drugs. Then, too, a brain tumor could have been responsible for her symptoms. In addition, her current state may have been a temporary, yet extreme, sign of the grief and sense of loss she felt because of her father's death. People in mourning often have *hallucinations*, sensory impressions that have no basis in reality.

Quite obviously, Nancy's overall behavior was markedly abnormal, but what exactly was the source of her problems? Many healthy young adults have tried drugs, have mental illness in their families, and have experienced the death of a close family member. What made Nancy different?

A trained psychiatric professional could certainly conclude that Nancy has a *psychosis*, a condition in which a

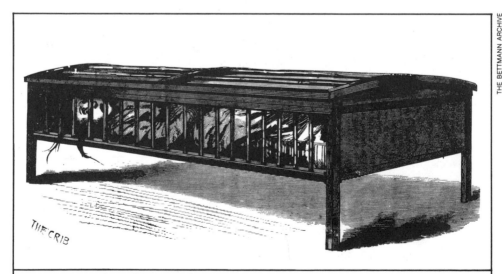

THE BETTMANN ARCHIVE

An 1880 woodcut shows an object known as the "crib," which was used in the Victorian period to restrain unmanageable victims of insanity. A variety of other traditional forms of restraint included straitjackets and manacles.

person's abilities to think, evaluate, communicate, remember, respond emotionally, and behave appropriately are so impaired that he or she is unable to cope with the ordinary demands of life. Nancy's symptoms also fit the description of *schizophrenia*, a mental disorder characterized by a loss of contact with reality. Late adolescence is frequently the time when the symptoms of this disorder first become evident.

In cases like Nancy's, special tests such as brain scans and blood tests, which are designed to measure metabolic imbalances, are necessary. Her doctor would probably also want to test her urine to determine whether she was using drugs which might be causing or heightening her psychosis. Once all the medical data had been analyzed and Nancy had been extensively interviewed, a psychiatrist would be ready to decide on a course of treatment. Such treatment might well include an antipsychotic drug if she were diagnosed as suffering from acute schizophrenia.

In past centuries the cruel and inhuman treatment of madness, as shown in this 18th-century sketch, reflected society's superstitions and fears regarding insanity, which was commonly perceived as the work of the devil.

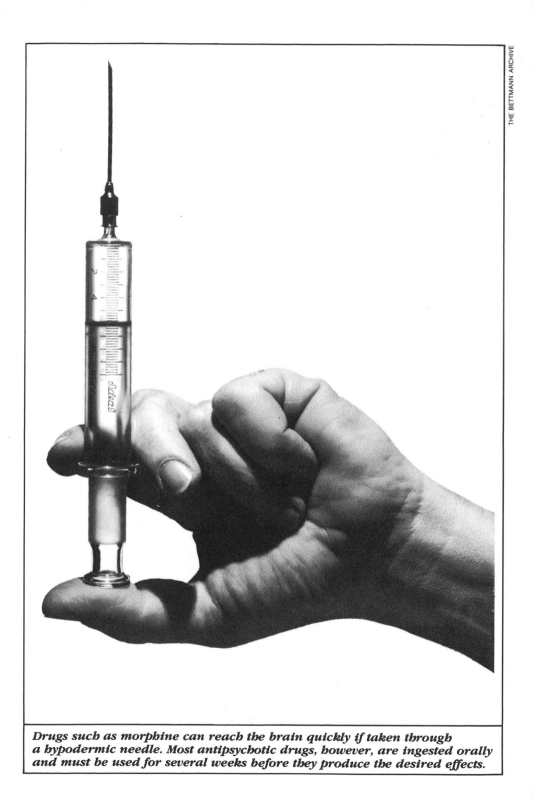

Drugs such as morphine can reach the brain quickly if taken through a hypodermic needle. Most antipsychotic drugs, however, are ingested orally and must be used for several weeks before they produce the desired effects.

CHAPTER 2

ANTIPSYCHOTIC DRUGS

*T*he original antipsychotic drugs all had chemical structures derived from phenothiazine. Researchers experimented
with many variations of the chemical structure of this molecule to see whether they had benefits and side effects similar
to chlorpromazine.

The most striking similarity among the antipsychotic
drugs was that all such compounds were dopamine-blocking
drugs. As we mentioned earlier, dopamine is a neurotransmitter — a chemical substance found in the brain that acts
as a transmitter of messages between nerve cells.

Scientists originally relied on behavioral testing of rats
to screen chemicals for antipsychotic activity, but present
methods involve direct testing for dopamine-blocking activity
in the brains of experimental animals. The discovery of dopamine-blocking activity has led doctors to believe that the
onset of schizophrenia is related to an abnormality in the
dopamine transmission system in the brain.

Schizophrenia is the most common of the psychoses, and
affects approximately one percent of the population in all

countries where statistics have been gathered. Although standards exist that define the disease, there is still some concern that it may not be one disease but rather several different diseases with common symptoms. Schizophrenia may occur in late adolescence or early adulthood in two apparently distinct forms. In one form, exemplified by Nancy in our first case history, the patient grows up normally until there is a fairly rapid degeneration of thought and behavior. In the other form, the patient is considered odd and asocial (withdrawn) from early childhood, and acute psychotic symptoms are superimposed on a long-standing withdrawn behavior pattern.

Schizophrenics do not have "split" personalities, and are not "dumb." In fact, they may be very intelligent, but because of their mental illness they cannot function successfully in their work situation. In the past, schizophrenics have been repeatedly hospitalized for psychiatric treatment. Today, for medical, humanitarian, and economic reasons, doctors and other psychiatric health care workers are trying to decrease the number and duration of hospital stays. One of the most impressive results of the drug treatment revolution in psychiatry has been the reduction of both the number of patients in mental hospitals and the average length of their stay.

Pharmacology

Eighteen antipsychotic drugs are presently available in the United States. Although they differ in their potency, all can be equally effective in the treatment of psychoses. On the other hand, their side effects can be very different. To help explain the pharmacology of the antipsychotics, chlorpromazine can be used as a model.

Chlorpromazine comes in three forms — as pills or capsules, in a liquid state for oral use, and in a liquid state for injections. How a drug is taken often determines how quickly it takes effect. Some drugs, such as chlorpromazine, are metabolized, or broken down, in the liver. When a drug is taken by mouth, it passes through the liver on its first trip through the bloodstream. When chlorpromazine is given by injection, however, much larger amounts may reach the brain before any metabolism occurs. An injected dose of chlorpromazine would therefore be smaller than a dose taken orally.

The first effect we often see in a patient taking chlorpromazine is sleepiness. All antipsychotic drugs have sedative, or tranquilizing, effects. Some drugs, such as chlorpromazine and thioridazine (Mellaril), are more likely than others to induce sedation in even the most anxious or agitated patients. In addition to its antipsychotic properties, chlorpromazine also helps to reduce nausea. When it is prescribed for this purpose to otherwise normal patients, its sedative property is seen as a side effect. Thus, whereas sedation is a therapeutic effect when chlorpromazine is used for treating psychiatric problems, it is a side effect when the drug is used to treat nausea.

In some patients with "organic brain syndrome," a psychotic condition caused by brain disease or tumors, chlorpromazine may decrease the thought disorder and agitation within a few hours. However, chlorpromazine and related drugs require repeated administration for weeks or months to produce their striking therapeutic changes in schizophrenic individuals.

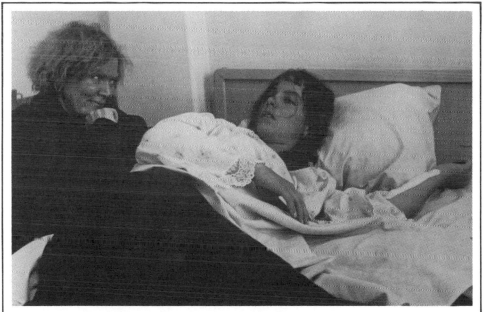

The 1977 movie I Never Promised You a Rose Garden *was based upon Hannah Green's autobiography and depicted how the author was cured of teenage schizophrenia through her relationship with a skilled psychiatrist.*

Side Effects

Chlorpromazine and, to a certain extent, all other antipsychotic drugs block a portion of the *sympathetic nervous system*, which controls the constriction of the blood vessels. (The sympathetic nervous system is part of the central nervous system, which controls involuntary bodily functions.) These drugs are called *alpha adrenergic blocking agents*, meaning that they have properties that can prevent the proper flow of blood and oxygen to the brain. Thus, patients who take these drugs may feel faint or dizzy when they stand up too quickly.

Chlorpromazine, acting like *atropine*, a substance naturally present in the body, is also a blocker of the *parasympathetic nervous system*. (This system controls involuntary activity such as sweating and contraction of the intestine.)

This painting, entitled Life Story, *was done by a schizophrenic patient with suicidal tendencies. Contrary to popular belief, many victims of schizophrenia are highly intelligent, but tend to see life as a collage of disassociated, and often frightening, impressions.*

Patients taking chlorpromazine and other antipsychotics often suffer from dry mouth and a decrease in perspiration. Older men, in particular, may experience difficulty with urination. Because of its resemblance to atropine, chlorpromazine is never given to patients who might have taken one of the hallucinogenic drugs that has atropine-like effects. It is also not given to patients whose psychosis has been caused by the use of PCP (phencyclidine, or angel dust, a dangerous drug that produces unpredictable effects, including stimulation, depression, and hallucinations). Some of the other antipsychotic drugs, such as fluphenazine (Prolixin), have less atropine-like effects.

Chlorpromazine and similar drugs also affect the body's hormone systems, partly as a result of the dopamine-blocking effect thought to produce the drug's therapeutic action. For example, non-nursing women who take chlorpromazine

A patient weaves a basket at a psychiatric hospital in Cuba. Hospitals will often combine drug therapy with individual, family, and group psychotherapy in order to help the patient cope with the outside world.

UPI/BETTMANN NEWSPHOTOS

sometimes start to secrete milk. The production of milk is normally prevented by the presence of the *prolactin inhibiting factor*, probably the neurotransmitter dopamine. But because chlorpromazine has a dopamine-blocking effect, the prolactin is stimulated and the body begins to lactate, or produce milk. Although *galactorrhea*, or the excessive flow of milk, can be a very disturbing side effect, it can be treated with other drugs.

Many antipsychotic drugs also cause *photosensitivity*, a condition in which the skin reacts abnormally to light. Patients who use these drugs should therefore apply a powerful sunscreen lotion before they go outside. Patients must also be aware of the fact that these drugs intensify the effects of alcohol. This makes it very hazardous for individuals using antipsychotic drugs to drink and drive a car or operate potentially dangerous machinery.

ART RESOURCE

Blurred vision is one of the unpleasant side effects of antipsychotic drugs. Other side effects include dry mouth, increase or decrease in perspiration, dizziness, and muscular weakness or rigidity.

Neurological Side Effects

The most striking side effect produced by chlorpromazine and other antipsychotic drugs is their influence on body control. Although these neurological reactions are common to all antipsychotic drugs, some medicines, such as thioridazine, are less likely than others, such as haloperidol, to cause these effects.

One serious neurological side effect includes a group of symptoms that closely resembles those associated with Parkinson's disease, an ailment most common among older people. Although the actual cause of the disease remains a

The precise role that psychiatric drugs play in the treatment of psychosis has not yet been determined. Physicians are kept abreast of developments in the field of drug therapy by a variety of medical journals.

mystery, we do know that Parkinson victims suffer a lack of dopamine in the nuclei of certain brain cells. Because the antipsychotics block dopamine, they produce Parkinson-like symptoms. These include fine tremors, a facial expressionlessness known as *Parkinson's mask*, and muscular weakness and rigidity. The tremor occurs only at rest, not during sleep or intentional movement. People suffering from this disease may jerk when they try to move their arms or legs, and in severe cases they may feel painfully stiff and experience difficulty walking. Parkinsonism is treated with L-DOPA, a chemical that is converted into dopamine in the brain. In some cases it has produced considerable improvement.

The feelings of helpless rage and entrapment sometimes experienced by victims of psychosis are powerfully evoked in this drawing by a schizophrenic mental patient. The discovery of antipsychotic drugs has revolutionized the treatment of schizophrenia.

Antipsychotic drugs also produce a condition called *akathisia*, the inability to sit still or maintain a resting posture. This side effect is confusing to both patient and doctor because the symptoms are frequently similar to the agitation caused by the patient's mental illness.

Occasionally, during the early stages of treatment with antipsychotics, a patient will have muscle spasms, often in the neck. Although this can be very frightening, this symptom can be treated successfully with an injection of certain drugs.

Tardive Dyskinesia

One additional neurological effect of antipsychotic-drug use, *tardive dyskinesia* (literally meaning "late-occurring difficulty with movement"), appears late in treatment. In most cases, a drug's side effects occur during drug treatment and disappear when treatment is stopped. Tardive dyskinesia, however, first appears well into the course of treatment, often when the dosage of the drug has been reduced. It appears

Cult leader Charles Manson was arrested and convicted in the brutal slaying of actress Sharon Tate and several of her associates in 1969. It is hoped that scientists can develop medication in the near future that can control the type of extreme psychosis that drove Manson and his "family" to commit such a horrible and senseless crime.

most often in older people and is more likely to occur following the administration of large doses of an antipsychotic drug over a long period of time. Unfortunately, when the drug is suddenly discontinued, the tardive dyskinesia remains and may never go away. Tardive dyskinesia is the major reason that doctors are cautious about prescribing antipsychotic drugs, all of which have an equal probability of causing this disorder.

The most common form of tardive dyskinesia is characterized by involuntary mouth movements that resemble chewing, sometimes accompanied by an in-and-out movement of the tongue. More severe forms of this disorder include slow, rhythmic, automatic movements of the arms and torso, which can be both disconcerting and disfiguring. A person suffering from tardive dyskinesia has no control over these movements, and unfortunately there is no effective treatment.

A therapy session at a hospital in Seattle. Although "talk therapies" alone have questionable value in the treatment of psychosis, they are often a valuable supplement when used in conjunction with antipsychotic drugs.

Obviously, patients should be warned that this irreversible side effect may occur as a result of treatment. In general, true tardive dyskinesia occurs after at least three months of drug treatment, although many patients take the drugs for years with no sign of this disorder. Although tardive dyskinesia is disfiguring, it is rarely life threatening. Psychosis, however, can totally disrupt an individual's life. Patients with tardive dyskinesia often choose to continue taking antipsychotic medicine because they are unable to function without it. If an antipsychotic drug can successfully treat this serious illness, the benefit is worth the risk.

Treating Side Effects with Drugs

The side effects caused by antipsychotic drugs are frequently treated with other drugs. The beneficial effects of antipsychotic drugs may not become apparent until weeks or even months after they are first taken, while most of their side effects occur almost immediately. Physicians therefore often find it necessary to minimize the negative effects by prescribing drugs that treat the side effects, so that patients will continue to take their medicine. After all, it does require an act of faith to take a medicine that may not produce its beneficial effects until months later.

Therapeutic Effects

The discovery of antipsychotic drugs has brought new hope to the treatment of schizophrenia. Successful drug treatment not only markedly decreases the patient's agitation and anxiety, but also relieves many of the major symptoms. Schizophrenics who have been treated for more than several weeks begin to think in a more organized manner. They reemerge from the private worlds they have created for themselves and start to reestablish contact with other people and with their surroundings. Patients who have undergone the new treatments appear more alive and active. They stop having delusions, and their hallucinations may completely disappear or persist in a much less disturbing form. The paranoia and feelings of being controlled by outside forces diminish. The treated patients gain a better sense of reality.

When manic, highly excited patients are treated with the antipsychotic drugs, their restlessness subsides, and their racing thoughts slow down. Since hostility often arises out of fear, the drugs' antianxiety properties often alleviate the manic patient's aggressiveness. (In contrast, the antianxiety or sedative properties of drugs like the barbiturates, benzodiazepines [antianxiety and sedative drugs, such as Valium], and alcohol often increase aggressiveness.) Without feeling as if they had been heavily sedated, patients begin to feel and act calmer. In addition, the antipsychotic drugs decrease the feelings of euphoric indifference, so that manic individuals once again begin to care about the consequences of their behavior.

The antipsychotic drugs do not produce sudden dramatic transformations, and not all of the changes occur in every patient. Sometimes a particular drug has little or no effect, making it necessary to try a different compound. Other times the dosage has to be adjusted to determine the optimal balance between therapeutic effects and side effects. Because of the nature of their illness, psychiatric patients are sometimes afraid that they are being poisoned and thus resist taking drugs. These feelings may be increased by the patients' understandable fear of the drugs' side effects.

Because of the many problems associated with taking and administering antipsychotic drugs, the treatment of psychosis requires an all-out, comprehensive effort on the part

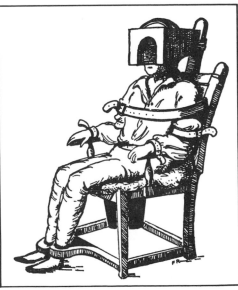

Before the discovery of antipsychotic drugs, such methods as this 18th-century "tranquilizing chair," which was designed by Dr. Benjamin Rush, were used for the treatment of violent mental patients. A signer of the Declaration of Independence, Rush was also an eminent physician who wrote several books exploring the mysteries of mental disease.

THE BETTMANN ARCHIVE

of everyone involved with the patient. Although drugs vastly improve psychotic patients' perception of their environment, patients must be helped to learn how to relate positively to this often bewildering "new world." To meet these demands, today's mental hospitals often combine drug therapy with individual, family, and group psychotherapy.

Schizophrenic patients can never be entirely cured of their disease. For this reason, to suppress the debilitating symptoms so that schizophrenics can function successfully outside an institution, long-term treatment with antipsychotic drugs may be required. In some cases, schizophrenic patients whose behavior has been stabilized by drugs may experience intermittent psychotic episodes. In other cases, even with drug treatment, the behavior of such patients may remain a bit strange. They are frequently unable to establish themselves socially and thus lead a marginal existence. Doctors must decide whether to keep the patient on a constant schedule of antipsychotic drugs or to administer them intermittently as the need arises. Because of the threat of tardive

THE BETTMANN ARCHIVE

An 1818 drawing of a circulating swing, which was used in attempts to bring patients out of deep depressions. Supposedly, the rotating and dizzying movements of the swing would somehow eliminate depression.

dyskinesia, doctors try to treat the mental illness by prescribing the smallest possible dosage to be taken intermittently.

Between episodes of their illness, manic-depressive people are frequently completely normal. The use of antipsychotic drugs to treat these patients is usually restricted to manic episodes, although chronic doses of lithium, a drug which we will discuss more fully, are often prescribed to prevent recurrences.

Other Treatments for Psychosis

Several forms of nondrug treatment have been both proposed and tried in order to help schizophrenic patients. Some radical theorists have proposed that instead of considering severely aberrant behavior to be a symptom of mental illness, we should simply accept and tolerate as different the individuals who exhibit these symptoms. Most mental health professionals reject this theory, seeing it as being unhelpful and even destructive to patients.

Another approach calls for treating psychosis with large doses of vitamins. However, when scientifically tested and evaluated, this treatment did not prove to have any thera-

This 18th-century cartoon shows mental patients suffering from hallucinations. Such terrifying distortions of reality frequently haunt psychotic patients. The ability to relieve this type of illness is one of the great boons of modern pharmacology.

THE BETTMANN ARCHIVE

peutic benefits. On the other hand, this "megavitamin" treatment is not likely to be harmful, unless it deprives the patient of other effective treatment.

Psychotherapy has questionable value in the treatment of acute psychosis. In fact, there is no evidence that it is any more effective than treatment with a *placebo*. (A placebo is a harmless pill made of a substance that is either pharmacologically inert or active only in the treatment of unrelated symptoms.) However, once the symptoms of psychosis have diminished, psychotherapy is successful in helping patients cope with the world.

Electroshock therapy (stimulating the brain with an electrical current to induce involuntary muscle contraction) is sometimes effective in treating agitated psychosis, but it is usually considered a measure of last resort. *Psychosurgery*, surgery performed on the brain, is rarely used today, although in certain cases it may be considered necessary.

The administration of antipsychotic drugs, often in conjunction with some form of psychotherapy, is now the most accepted form of treatment for psychosis. These treatments together make it possible for people who suffer from psychosis to function much more successfully in society.

In the Academy Award-winning movie One Flew Over the Cuckoo's Nest *(1975), Jack Nicholson (center) portrays a man who feigns insanity to avoid prison. Unfortunately, the strategy backfires and he is forced to submit to such treatment as electroshock therapy, and, finally, a pre-frontal lobotomy.*

Within the image: MELENCOLIA§I

Melancholia, *a work by the famous 16th-century German painter and engraver Albrecht Dürer, depicts the artist's symbolic view of depression, a condition that is characterized by feelings of despondency and sadness and has affected people throughout the ages.*

CHAPTER 3

DEPRESSION

Depression is not an easy concept to define. The word is used to describe a mood and a syndrome, as well as a mental disorder. The mood is characterized by feelings of despondency, sadness, and discouragement and is only one symptom of the mental disorder. When the mood persists, a syndrome of associated symptoms may arise, including diminished appetite, slowed thinking, a loss of interest in the world, and feelings of guilt and hopelessness that are associated with a depressed mood.

The mental disorder (or disease) of depression is one of the most common psychiatric illnesses. It is classified as an *affective disorder*, or a disorder that alters an individual's expression of his or her *mood state*. Mood state refers to a prolonged emotion that affects one's entire emotional life. Depression is not merely sadness; it is a serious emotional disease that can render people unable to function, ruin their relationships with others, and even lead to suicide.

Harry: A Case Study

Harry was 46 years old, happily married, and successfully employed as an accountant until his only daughter left home to go to college. For the first time in many years, Harry found himself all alone with his wife. He missed his daughter and began to have difficulty concentrating at work. He became increasingly irritable with his colleagues and his wife. Harry lost interest in food, stopped eating dinner, and lost 12 pounds. Despite the fact that he was tired all the time, he could not sleep. He began to think he was a failure at his job, and fantasized about suicide.

Painful personal crises can trigger deep depressions, which can lead to thoughts of suicide. This is especially true for those who are psychologically or biochemically predisposed to this affliction. Psychiatrists are particularly inclined to prescribe antidepressant drugs to a patient who is potentially suicidal.

THE BETTMANN ARCHIVE

It was obvious that Harry was sad. His face showed little expression and when he moved, it was in a painfully slow manner. No matter what his wife did to try to cheer him up, he felt as if he could never again find any pleasure in his life.

Harry had experienced a similar, though less severe, episode of depression at age 27. That episode, however, had lasted only three months before the pervasive feelings of sadness had completely disappeared.

The fact that Harry exhibited both mental and physical symptoms seemed to indicate that he was not merely unhappy that his daughter had left home, but that he was suffering from some sort of psychiatric disorder. Before he was diagnosed as depressed, however, the possibility of physical illness had to be ruled out. Cancer, thyroid imbalance, and some neurological diseases produce symptoms similar to those characteristic of depression. Once the necessary tests had been evaluated, a psychiatrist was able to diagnose Harry's illness as depression. Depression is an especially dangerous illness because it often carries the risk of suicide. Harry had to be evaluated to determine whether he might commit suicide, and whether hospitalization might therefore be necessary. Whatever the decision, Harry's psychiatrist, in conjunction with Harry, also had to decide whether to treat him with antidepressant drugs and, if so, what kind.

Art therapy is sometimes used to supplement drugs and psychotherapy in the treatment of mental illness. This elderly woman found that by making drawings of her inner "demons," she was able to dispel the terror they held for her.

The History of Treating Depression with Drugs

Prior to the 1950s, the anxiety and sleeplessness that often accompany depression could be treated only with sedatives, which took care of the symptoms but not the source of the disease. In 1957 the Swiss psychiatrist Roland Kuhn administered *imipramine* (a drug that resembles phenothiazine and which was originally created for its antihistamine and sedative properties) to various psychiatric patients. He noticed that although imipramine had no therapeutic effect on psychotic patients, depressed patients did respond positively to the drug after a few weeks of treatment.

In the years that followed, other scientists noticed that tuberculosis patients who were treated with the drug *iproniazid* also seemed to recover from depression. This observation led to the discovery of the group of antidepressants called *monoamine oxidase inhibitors* (see below).

The Chemical Basis of Depression

Soon after the development of antidepressant drugs, scientists developed a theory of how they worked. They already knew that reserpine (the antipsychotic and blood-pressure-lowering drug derived from the snakeroot plant of India) caused depression in some patients. Biochemical studies had shown that reserpine caused a release of amines (a type of chemical compound) in the brain that *decreased* the amount of neurotransmitters available for the transmission of information between nerves.

Experiments on animals demonstrated that all of the drugs that had antidepressant properties *increased* the amount of amine neurotransmitters in the brain. Different antidepressants did this in different ways. The tricyclic antidepressants stopped the amines from being recycled, so that an excess of the neurotransmitters built up at the nerve endings. The monoamine oxidase inhibitors stopped the action of monoamine oxidase, which breaks down the amine transmitters, and thus also allowed a buildup of the neurotransmitters. From this information scientists hypothesized that depression was the result of a decrease in these amine transmitters in some part of the brain.

Since this hypothesis was formulated, additional data have shown this initial explanation of depression and the action of antidepressant drugs to be an oversimplification. Although in general the description is probably accurate, some drugs do not fit the theory, and there is still no adequate explanation of why all antidepressants take two weeks or more to produce their beneficial effects.

We need to remember that although depression is caused by chemical changes in the brain, these changes can be triggered by psychological factors. Sometimes, even when a person shows symptoms of the disease, we do not consider him or her clinically depressed (needing treatment). For example, people who suffer a great loss go through a period of mourning, frequently exhibiting all the symptoms of depression. However, mourning is considered a natural part of one's psychological life. Unlike true depression, it has a predictable course. Total recovery almost always occurs within several months without the use of drugs.

A painting by Robert Fleury shows French physician Philippe Pinel unchaining mentally ill patients. Pinel was one of the first to think that insanity resulted from physiological causes rather than possession by demons.

Drug Treatment

Two major groups of drugs are used to treat depression. The first group, which was mentioned previously, is the tricyclic antidepressants. The discussion of this group of drugs, however, will include some drugs that have different chemical structures but exhibit similar actions and side effects. The

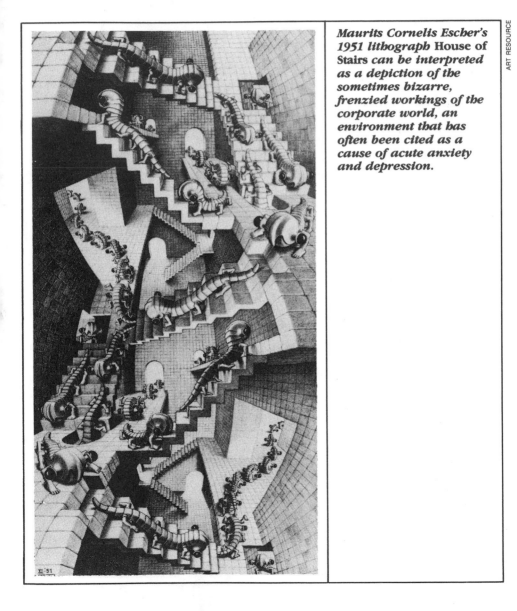

Maurits Cornelis Escher's 1951 lithograph House of Stairs *can be interpreted as a depiction of the sometimes bizarre, frenzied workings of the corporate world, an environment that has often been cited as a cause of acute anxiety and depression.*

ART RESOURCE

first tricyclic drug discovered, imipramine, can serve to illustrate this group of drugs.

Imipramine, like chlorpromazine, has *antihistaminic* effects, that is, it inhibits the action of histamine in the body, and thus reduces the allergic response. (Allergy pills and cold pills often include antihistamines.) Imipramine also has atropine-like effects, which means that it causes dry mouth, widened pupils, and urinary hesitancy. None of these actions seem to be necessary for imipramine's antidepressant effect.

A patient who takes imipramine, usually in the form of a pill or capsule, may first react by feeling sleepy. Although drowsiness is actually a side effect, it can be quite useful. Depression in any serious form is almost always accompanied by a disturbance in sleep. Some people cannot sleep at all, while others sleep too much. Imipramine will often remedy these problems in a day or so. A sleeping pill could also relieve the sleeplessness, but it would not treat the depression.

Imipramine and most other tricyclics prevent blood vessels from constricting normally, and can thus cause *postural hypotension* (a decrease in blood pressure during a change in body position). Patients may experience dizziness when they stand up, the result of blood suddenly draining into the legs and causing a lack of blood in the brain. Patients are cautioned to stand up very slowly.

As mentioned earlier, one of the most serious problems in antidepressant treatment is that patients may suffer side effects almost immediately, without feeling the therapeutic benefits until they have taken the drug for several weeks. However, about a week after the therapeutic dose is reached, the depression lifts. The patients' images of themselves become more realistic, and their view of the world seems less bleak. They are able to concentrate, sleep better, and feel "blue" less often. As their feelings of desperation and despair lessen, the idea of suicide fades.

Although the improvements come on slowly, in successful cases the patient's depression disappears within a month. Over three-quarters of patients suffering serious depressions can be helped significantly with the antidepressant drugs. Not all patients respond equally well to all the drugs. Doctors often need to test a patient's reactions to one or two different drugs before they can determine the most effective medicine for the patient.

Monoamine Oxidase Inhibitors

A patient who does not respond to the tricyclic antidepressants and similar drugs may try the *monoamine oxidase inhibitors*. Monoamine oxidase is an *enzyme* (an organic compound that induces chemical changes in other substances without being changed itself) that normally breaks down amines in the brain. When monoamine oxidase does not work properly, the amines accumulate in the brain. All the antidepressant drugs, including the drugs that inhibit the effect of the monoamine oxidase, produce a buildup of amines.

Although the monoamine oxidase inhibitors are often strikingly effective in treating depression, they can also cause serious side effects. Besides breaking down brain amines, monoamine oxidase has a number of other functions in the body. In the liver and intestines, monoamine oxidase breaks up some of the *amino acids* (the basic elements of all proteins) which we get from food. Certain amino acids in foods, such as tyramine, have the potential to act as a drug on the heart and the blood vessels to increase blood pressure. Ordinarily, monoamine oxidase breaks up the tyramine before it can produce this effect. When monoamine oxidase is inhibited, however, the tyramine causes a release of naturally occurring amines. A serious, and even damaging, increase in blood pressure and subsequent stroke or heart attack can result.

When a person taking a monoamine oxidase inhibitor eats a tyramine-containing food, such as beer, wine, most cheeses, and chicken liver, his or her blood pressure may rise suddenly. Doctors therefore stress that such patients must absolutely avoid the tyramine-containing foods. Because monoamine oxidase inhibitors also interact with some medicines, patients must check with their doctors before taking any other drugs.

Three monoamine oxidase inhibitors are used as antidepressants. They all have similar therapeutic effects and negative side effects. Phenelzine (Nardil), a representative of the group, may be prescribed for a depressed patient who does not respond to treatment with a tricyclic drug. Because the tricyclics and the monoamine oxidase inhibitors interact, the patient must wait at least a week between the last dose of tricyclic and the first treatment with phenelzine. Doctors must, of course, be careful to warn their patients about phe-nelzine's potentially dangerous interactions with foods and other drugs.

Patients taking phenelzine may experience dizziness, a result of the drug's blood-pressure-lowering effect. They may or may not get relief from whatever sleeping problems they are having. They may not notice the drug's full antidepressant effect for about two weeks, a delay which may be difficult for the patient. But, as with the tricyclics, after a period of time the drug's positive effects become apparent. The patient begins to enjoy life again, and experiences an improvement in his or her ability to concentrate. All the symptoms of the depression eventually disappear. Patients often continue to take these drugs for six months to a year, until the doctor is sure that the underlying disease has abated.

Some victims of clinical depression, which often has its roots in earliest childhood and can last a lifetime, can now control their affliction by taking prescribed dosages of tricyclic antidepressants, such as imipramine.

The monoamine oxidase inhibitors are usually the second choice of treatment and should be used only with patients who can be absolutely trusted to monitor their diet. Because there is a wide range of drug interactions, patients who require the use of drugs other than the monoamine oxidase inhibitors must be treated very carefully. For appropriate patients, however, the monoamine oxidase inhibitors are safe and effective.

Other Treatments for Depression

Depression can also be treated with electroconvulsive shock. Although it has gained a negative reputation, this form of therapy is the most consistently effective treatment for depression. Today, however, most psychiatrists reserve it for treating patients who do not respond to drugs.

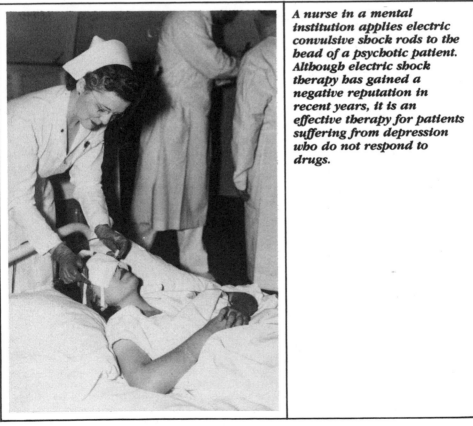

A nurse in a mental institution applies electric convulsive shock rods to the head of a psychotic patient. Although electric shock therapy has gained a negative reputation in recent years, it is an effective therapy for patients suffering from depression who do not respond to drugs.

AP/WIDE WORLD PHOTOS

Psychotherapy is a successful form of treatment for many mild depressions. Patients are more often treated with psychotherapy when the causes of the depression seem related to life crises, or to an inability to adjust or cope with the social environment. The use of antidepressant drugs is usually considered (1) if the depressed patient does not respond at all to psychotherapy within about ten visits; (2) if for over two weeks the patient has difficulty functioning and suffers from such physical symptoms as weight loss and serious sleep disturbance; and (3) if a patient exhibits suicidal tendencies, in which case hospitalization should also be considered.

The Pulitzer Prize-winning poet Anne Sexton holds her book Live or Die, *the title of which prophetically projected a challenge she faced during a series of depressions, culminating in her suicide in 1974.*

Extreme mood swings characterize manic depressives, people whose emotional states alternate between exaggerated feelings of well-being and severe depression. Anti-psychotic drugs are used to stabilize these moods and bring patients towards gradual recovery.

CHAPTER 4

MANIC-DEPRESSIVE PSYCHOSIS

ne of the most serious psychiatric diseases is manic-depressive psychosis. Patients with this disease may have episodes of mania only, when they feel abnormally excited and have exaggerated feelings of well-being, or alternating episodes of mania and depression. In between these extreme mood swings, patients are often completely normal.

Andrew: A Case Study

Andrew, a 28-year-old, single computer programmer, came into his doctor's office looking very excited. Speaking quickly, jumping from topic to topic with great enthusiasm, he told the doctor that he had just written the most important computer program ever developed. The doctor questioned him about this program, whereupon Andrew became very irritable and suspicious. As he paced about the office, he explained that the Japanese had been trying to steal his secrets. He had even telephoned various people in Japan to question them about their involvement in computer theft, and his phone bills were five times higher than normal. In the middle of his story he suddenly started to cry, but just as quickly he cheered up again and described the new company he was planning to establish with money from friends. He told the doctor he had been giving elaborate gifts to everyone he knew, "to reward them for their support."

Andrew's expansive mood, his irritability, and his quick mood shifts are all typical of what psychiatrists call "mania." Patients who suffer from this illness may not be happy or euphoric, but their mood state is always expansive. They sleep very little and can even die from exhaustion. They frequently squander money and alienate friends. Severe paranoia and aggressiveness are common.

The History of Treating Manic-Depressives

Before the development of effective drug treatment, manic patients were more difficult to control than any other group among the mentally ill. They rode a dangerous roller coaster through life, sometimes swinging rapidly from the heights of mania to the extreme depths of depression. Before 1950, ineffective sleep therapies and shock treatments were the only methods available for the treatment of mania.

In 1949 Dr. John Cade began to study the basis of mania. Thinking that some toxin secreted by the body might induce the manic state, he compared the urine of manic patients to that of other patients. In laboratory experiments with guinea

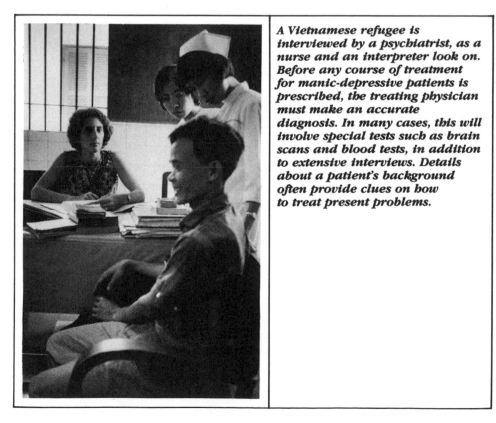

A Vietnamese refugee is interviewed by a psychiatrist, as a nurse and an interpreter look on. Before any course of treatment for manic-depressive patients is prescribed, the treating physician must make an accurate diagnosis. In many cases, this will involve special tests such as brain scans and blood tests, in addition to extensive interviews. Details about a patient's background often provide clues on how to treat present problems.

UPI/BETTMANN NEWSPHOTOS

pigs, he discovered that the urine from manic patients was, in fact, more toxic than other urine. The toxic substance appeared to be a *urate*, a chemical normally found in urine, but in smaller quantities.

Cade already knew that lithium binds, or combines, with urates to produce lithium urate, a compound that will readily dissolve in water. Therefore, he hypothesized, administering lithium to the animals might protect them from the toxic effects of the urates. In fact, he discovered that not only did lithium protect the animals, but it also seemed to sedate them. His next step was to try the lithium on manic patients. Within a few days of administering the drug, Cade noted that the mania abated, and over the course of a few weeks, it entirely disappeared.

Although further research showed that Cade was wrong about *how* lithium worked, he had discovered an effective substance to treat mania. Cade's success was reported in a

Finding healthy ways to deal with anger is often one of the keys to mental health. Although manic-depressive illness has not been specifically linked to environmental factors, it is known that if it is not properly vented, unreasonable anger in children can lead to a lifetime of problematic emotional duress.

paper published in the *Medical Journal of Australia*, but unlike the medical profession's immediate positive response to chlorpromazine, this report was received unenthusiastically. Not until 20 years later was the discovery of lithium recognized. Today, lithium is an accepted medicine for the prevention of recurrent manic episodes, for the treatment of acute mania, and for the treatment of depression in manic-depressive patients.

The Psychopharmacology of Lithium

Lithium is a chemical element that occurs in nature as a white metal. In medicine, lithium is used in the form of a carbonate salt (combined with the compound H_2CO_3). Therefore, the term lithium actually refers to lithium carbonate. Though rather simple in structure, lithium has very complex actions in the body. The exact basis for these actions is still unknown.

Although lithium is not normally found in the body, it resembles both sodium and potassium, chemicals that are

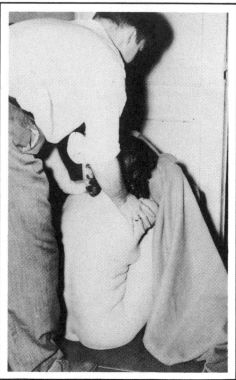

This woman, who was diagnosed as being both drunk and manic, disrobed on top of a truck in Dallas midday traffic. It has not been proven what the causes of manic-depressive psychosis are, but according to some theories, it is a genetic disorder, and most of its victims are in their 30s or 40s.

AP/WIDE WORLD PHOTOS

necessary for the functioning of all the body's nerves. To some degree, lithium is able to substitute for sodium and potassium.

Lithium increases an individual's white blood cell count, and therefore is sometimes used to help people who have low "white counts" owing to cancer-treatment drugs. And finally, the drug affects the functioning of the brain, perhaps because of its ability to alter the brain's amine balance.

Like other psychotherapeutic drugs, lithium takes some time to produce its therapeutic effect. When patients first begin taking the drug they may experience fine tremors of the hands and an increase in both thirst and urination. Lithium may also affect the thyroid gland (a gland located in the neck that produces a hormone that affects growth, development, and metabolic rate). It can cause a reversible *goiter* (an enlargement of the thyroid gland that produces symptoms such as bulging eyeballs, tremors of the fingers and hands, and an increase in metabolic rate) or *hypothyroidism* (a decrease in thyroid secretions that causes a lowered metabolic rate

Blood is drawn to test for levels of lithium, a salt-like mineral used to control — and prevent — maniacal episodes. In 1949 the Australian psychiatrist John Cade discovered that lithium could be used to treat mania, but it took 20 years before the importance of his discovery was fully recognized.

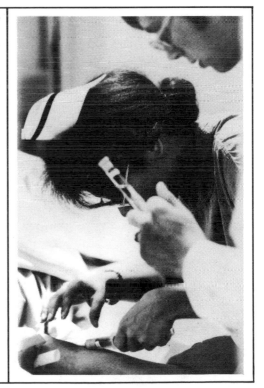

and such symptoms as obesity, low blood pressure and pulse, and depressed muscular activity). Because lithium is often used to *prevent* illness, doctors must keep in mind that in healthy individuals lithium produces tremors and increased urination, and can have a slight sedating effect, which is rarely considered unpleasant.

In manic patients, lithium is considered a mood-stabilizing drug. It slowly decreases irritability, aggressiveness, and the rapid flowing of ideas, and reduces the patient's expansive mood. It also decreases paranoia and, if hallucinations are present, they disappear. Lithium can have remarkable effects on anger and aggressiveness, and on such recurring diseases as *periodic catatonia*, a rare syndrome of repeated episodes of rigidity and loss of speech. Although lithium acts like an antipsychotic drug in its effect on mania, it has no effect on most other psychoses. This seems to indicate a common chemical basis for a whole pattern of symptoms. Despite this tantalizing lead, scientists are still mystified as to what is the chemical basis of manic-depressive psychosis.

Lithium is quickly absorbed from the stomach and distributed throughout the body. Patients must therefore almost always take the drug in several doses during the day. (It thus differs from the antidepressant and antipsychotic drugs, which can be taken in one daily dose at bedtime.) Because only a narrow margin exists between the therapeutic dose of lithium and the amount that can bring on toxic symptoms, patients taking lithium regularly undergo blood tests to monitor the level of the drug in their blood. These tests also help doctors determine whether the drug is being taken properly and whether the dosage is correct.

As the sodium level in the body decreases, the lithium level increases. When the lithium level gets too high, a patient may become confused and suffer from nausea and diarrhea. In order to avoid these symptoms, patients who take lithium and do strenuous physical work or exercise should supplement their diet with salt pills. They should also avoid low-sodium diets.

Manic-depressive psychosis very often cannot be cured, and many patients continue to be treated with lithium all their lives. In the past some doctors believed that long-term lithium treatment could damage the kidneys. However, current opinion is that as long as the patient's urine is analyzed periodically, lithium may be taken on a long-term basis. As discussed earlier, lithium can also adversely affect the thyroid gland, and patients on lithium must be tested regularly to ensure that the thyroid is functioning properly.

Because not all patients respond positively to lithium treatments, and a few cannot tolerate the side effects, a number of new drugs are being studied. The most promising of these is *carbamazepine* (Tegretol), a drug used in the treatment of epilepsy. Carbamazepine in many ways resembles lithium in its pharmacologic action. It has been found effective in treating mania and in preventing recurrent manic illness. However, because of the serious side effects sometimes produced by this drug (blood-cell abnormalities, heart failure, dizziness, blurred vision, fever, and vomiting), carbamazepine is used as a second choice, after the safer drugs have proven to be ineffective or inappropriate.

People who take lithium and exercise strenuously should supplement their diets with salt pills. This is because the loss of sodium that heavy perspiration causes, coupled with rising levels of lithium in the body, can lead to some serious and unpleasant side effects.

A psychiatrist examines the results of a sleep survey, which will enable him to predict which of several available antidepressant drugs will be the most effective one for his patient.

CHAPTER 5

THE FUTURE

*U*ntil recently, drugs that have proven effective in treating mental illness were discovered by scientists and doctors whose research and clinical experience alerted them to the psychiatric potential of a particular substance. By modifying the molecular structure of the original chemical they were then able to develop additional drugs. Because we do not have any adequate animal models of mental illness, we have been restricted in the development of new drugs.

The discovery of psychotherapeutic drugs has led to research into the amine systems of the brain, which, in turn, has provided more information about the chemistry of the brain. Newer techniques, such as PET scanning (a method by which radioactive isotopes are used to visualize the brain's chemistry), and Magnetic Resonance Imaging (a technique that uses giant magnets to create images of the anatomy of the brain and determine its chemistry), give us hope that in the future we will be able to visualize how mental illness alters the brain's chemistry. With this information, researchers will be able to design new drugs to correct abnormal chemical states and thus effectively treat mental disease.

Even though we know that mental illness has a chemical basis, we must not ignore the psychological dimensions of the disease. Drugs can be only one aspect of the treatment program for mental illness. Mental health professionals must also pay close attention to the complex needs and emotions of every patient in order to help that individual achieve a stronger sense of self and a healthier means of relating to his or her environment.

APPENDIX 1

SYMPTOMS OF CLINICAL DEPRESSION

A. Dysphoric mood, which is characterized by a loss of interest or pleasure in all or almost all usual activities and pastimes. Someone suffering from dysphoric mood might say that he or she feels depressed, sad, blue, hopeless, low, or down in the dumps. The mood disturbance must be prominent and relatively persistent, but not necessarily the most dominant symptom, and it does not include momentary shifts from one dysphoric mood to another dysphoric mood (e.g., anxiety to depression to anger), such as are seen in states of acute psychotic turmoil.

B. At least four of the following symptoms will each be present nearly every day for a period of at least two weeks:

    1. Poor appetite or significant weight loss (even though the person is not dieting) *or* increased appetite or significant weight gain

    2. Insomnia or, conversely, hypersomnia (sleeping for extreme periods of time)

    3. Psychomotor agitation or retardation (not merely subjective feelings of restlessness or being "slowed down")

    4. Loss of interest or pleasure in usual activities; decrease in sexual drive

    5. Loss of energy; fatigue

    6. Feelings of worthlessness, self-reproach, or excessive or inappropriate guilt

    7. Complaints or evidence of diminished ability to think or concentrate

    8. Recurrent thoughts of death and suicide, a desire to be dead, or an attempt at suicide

APPENDIX 2

SYMPTOMS OF MANIA

A. One or more distinct periods with a predominantly elevated, expansive, or irritable mood. The elevated or irritable mood must be a prominent part of the illness and relatively persistent, although it may alternate or intermingle with depressive mood.

B. Duration of at least one week during which at least three of the following symptoms persist and are present to a significant degree:

1. Increase in activity (either socially, at work, or sexually) or physical restlessness

2. Increased talkativeness

3. A subjective experience that thoughts are racing

4. Inflated self-esteem (grandiosity, which may be delusional)

5. Decreased need for sleep

6. Distractibility (i.e., attention too easily drawn to unimportant or irrelevant external stimuli)

7. Excessive involvement in activities that have a high potential for painful consequences, a risk which is not recognized by the person; activities can include buying sprees, sexual indiscretions, foolish business investments, and reckless driving

APPENDIX 3

SYMPTOMS OF SCHIZOPHRENIA

A. At least one of the following during a phase of the illness:

    1. Bizarre delusions (content is patently absurd and has *no* possible basis in fact, such as delusions of being controlled, thought broadcasting, thought insertion, or thought withdrawal)

    2. Grandiose, religious, nihilistic, or other delusions

    3. Delusions with persecutory or jealous content, if accompanied by hallucinations of any type

    4. Auditory hallucinations in which either a voice keeps up a running commentary on the individual's behavior or thoughts, or two or more voices converse with each other

    5. Auditory hallucinations on several occasions with content having no apparent relation to depression or elation

    6. Incoherence, marked loosening of associations, markedly illogical thinking, or marked poverty of content of speech if associated with at least one of the following:

    a. Apathy, or lack of involvement with the world

    b. Delusions or hallucinations

    c. Catatonic or other grossly disorganized behavior

B. Deterioration from a previous level of functioning in such areas as work, social relations, and self-care.

C. Duration: continuous signs of the illness for at least six months at some time during the person's life, with some signs of the illness at present.

D. At least two of the following symptoms:

    1. Social isolation or withdrawal

    2. Marked impairment in role functioning as wage earner, student, and/or homeworker

    3. Markedly peculiar behavior (e.g., collecting garbage, talking to self in public, hoarding food)

    4. Marked impairment in personal hygiene and grooming

5. Apathetic appearance

6. Digressive, vague, overelaborate, circumstantial, or metaphorical speech

7. Odd or bizarre thought processes (e.g., superstitiousness, or fantasies of clairvoyance or telepathy)

8. Unusual perceptual experiences (e.g., recurrent illusions, sensing the presence of a force or person not actually present)

APPENDIX 4

STATE AGENCIES FOR THE PREVENTION AND TREATMENT OF DRUG ABUSE

ALABAMA
Department of Mental Health
Division of Mental Illness and
  Substance Abuse Community
  Programs
200 Interstate Park Drive
P.O. Box 3710
Montgomery, AL 36193
(205) 271-9253

ALASKA
Department of Health and Social
  Services
Office of Alcoholism and Drug
  Abuse
Pouch H-05-F
Juneau, AK 99811
(907) 586-6201

ARIZONA
Department of Health Services
Division of Behavioral Health
  Services
Bureau of Community Services
Alcohol Abuse and Alcoholism
  Section
2500 East Van Buren
Phoenix, AZ 85008
(602) 255-1238

Department of Health Services
Division of Behavioral Health
  Services
Bureau of Community Services
Drug Abuse Section
2500 East Van Buren
Phoenix, AZ 85008
(602) 255-1240

ARKANSAS
Department of Human Services
Office on Alcohol and Drug Abuse
  Prevention
1515 West 7th Avenue
Suite 310
Little Rock, AR 72202
(501) 371-2603

CALIFORNIA
Department of Alcohol and Drug
  Abuse
111 Capitol Mall
Sacramento, CA 95814
(916) 445-1940

COLORADO
Department of Health
Alcohol and Drug Abuse Division
4210 East 11th Avenue
Denver, CO 80220
(303) 320-6137

CONNECTICUT
Alcohol and Drug Abuse
  Commission
999 Asylum Avenue
3rd Floor
Hartford, CT 06105
(203) 566-4145

DELAWARE
Division of Mental Health
Bureau of Alcoholism and Drug
  Abuse
1901 North Dupont Highway
Newcastle, DE 19720
(302) 421-6101

DISTRICT OF COLUMBIA
Department of Human Services
Office of Health Planning and
  Development
601 Indiana Avenue, NW
Suite 500
Washington, D.C. 20004
(202) 724-5641

FLORIDA
Department of Health and
  Rehabilitative Services
Alcoholic Rehabilitation Program
1317 Winewood Boulevard
Room 187A
Tallahassee, FL 32301
(904) 488-0396

Department of Health and
  Rehabilitative Services
Drug Abuse Program
1317 Winewood Boulevard
Building 6, Room 155
Tallahassee, FL 32301
(904) 488-0900

GEORGIA
Department of Human Resources
Division of Mental Health and
  Mental Retardation
Alcohol and Drug Section
618 Ponce De Leon Avenue, NE
Atlanta, GA 30365-2101
(404) 894-4785

HAWAII
Department of Health
Mental Health Division
Alcohol and Drug Abuse Branch
1250 Punch Bowl Street
P.O. Box 3378
Honolulu, HI 96801
(808) 548-4280

IDAHO
Department of Health and Welfare
Bureau of Preventive Medicine
Substance Abuse Section
450 West State
Boise, ID 83720
(208) 334-4368

ILLINOIS
Department of Mental Health and
  Developmental Disabilities
Division of Alcoholism
160 North La Salle Street
Room 1500
Chicago, IL 60601
(312) 793-2907

Illinois Dangerous Drugs
  Commission
300 North State Street
Suite 1500
Chicago, IL 60610
(312) 822-9860

INDIANA
Department of Mental Health
Division of Addiction Services
429 North Pennsylvania Street
Indianapolis, IN 46204
(317) 232-7816

IOWA
Department of Substance Abuse
505 5th Avenue
Insurance Exchange Building
Suite 202
Des Moines, IA 50319
(515) 281-3641

KANSAS
Department of Social Rehabilitation
Alcohol and Drug Abuse Services
2700 West 6th Street
Biddle Building
Topeka, KS 66606
(913) 296-3925

KENTUCKY
Cabinet for Human Resources
Department of Health Services
Substance Abuse Branch
275 East Main Street
Frankfort, KY 40601
(502) 564-2880

LOUISIANA
Department of Health and Human
  Resources
Office of Mental Health and
  Substance Abuse
655 North 5th Street
P.O. Box 4049
Baton Rouge, LA 70821
(504) 342-2565

MAINE
Department of Human Services
Office of Alcoholism and Drug
  Abuse Prevention
Bureau of Rehabilitation
32 Winthrop Street
Augusta, ME 04330
(207) 289-2781

MARYLAND
Alcoholism Control Administration
201 West Preston Street
Fourth Floor
Baltimore, MD 21201
(301) 383-2977

State Health Department
Drug Abuse Administration
201 West Preston Street
Baltimore, MD 21201
(301) 383-3312

MASSACHUSETTS
Department of Public Health
Division of Alcoholism
755 Boylston Street
Sixth Floor
Boston, MA 02116
(617) 727-1960

Department of Public Health
Division of Drug Rehabilitation
600 Washington Street
Boston, MA 02114
(617) 727-8617

MICHIGAN
Department of Public Health
Office of Substance Abuse Services
3500 North Logan Street
P.O. Box 30035
Lansing, MI 48909
(517) 373-8603

MINNESOTA
Department of Public Welfare
Chemical Dependency Program
  Division
Centennial Building
658 Cedar Street
4th Floor
Saint Paul, MN 55155
(612) 296-4614

MISSISSIPPI
Department of Mental Health
Division of Alcohol and Drug Abuse
1102 Robert E. Lee Building
Jackson, MS 39201
(601) 359-1297

MISSOURI
Department of Mental Health
Division of Alcoholism and Drug
  Abuse
2002 Missouri Boulevard
P.O. Box 687
Jefferson City, MO 65102
(314) 751-4942

MONTANA
Department of Institutions
Alcohol and Drug Abuse Division
1539 11th Avenue
Helena, MT 59620
(406) 449-2827

NEBRASKA
Department of Public Institutions
Division of Alcoholism and Drug Abuse
801 West Van Dorn Street
P.O. Box 94728
Lincoln, NB 68509
(402) 471-2851, Ext. 415

NEVADA
Department of Human Resources
Bureau of Alcohol and Drug Abuse
505 East King Street
Carson City, NV 89710
(702) 885-4790

NEW HAMPSHIRE
Department of Health and Welfare
Office of Alcohol and Drug Abuse
  Prevention
Hazen Drive
Health and Welfare Building
Concord, NH 03301
(603) 271-4627

NEW JERSEY
Department of Health
Division of Alcoholism
129 East Hanover Street CN 362
Trenton, NJ 08625
(609) 292-8949

Department of Health
Division of Narcotic and Drug Abuse
  Control
129 East Hanover Street CN 362
Trenton, NJ 08625
(609) 292-8949

NEW MEXICO
Health and Environment Department
Behavioral Services Division
Substance Abuse Bureau
725 Saint Michaels Drive
P.O. Box 968
Santa Fe, NM 87503
(505) 984-0020, Ext. 304

NEW YORK
Division of Alcoholism and Alcohol
  Abuse
194 Washington Avenue
Albany, NY 12210
(518) 474-5417

Division of Substance Abuse
  Services
Executive Park South
Box 8200
Albany, NY 12203
(518) 457-7629

NORTH CAROLINA
Department of Human Resources
Division of Mental Health, Mental
  Retardation and Substance Abuse
  Services
Alcohol and Drug Abuse Services
325 North Salisbury Street
Albemarle Building
Raleigh, NC 27611
(919) 733-4670

NORTH DAKOTA
Department of Human Services
Division of Alcoholism and Drug
  Abuse
State Capitol Building
Bismarck, ND 58505
(701) 224-2767

OHIO
Department of Health
Division of Alcoholism
246 North High Street
P.O. Box 118
Columbus, OH 43216
(614) 466-3543

Department of Mental Health
Bureau of Drug Abuse
65 South Front Street
Columbus, OH 43215
(614) 466-9023

OKLAHOMA
Department of Mental Health
Alcohol and Drug Programs
4545 North Lincoln Boulevard
Suite 100 East Terrace
P.O. Box 53277
Oklahoma City, OK 73152
(405) 521-0044

OREGON
Department of Human Resources
Mental Health Division
Office of Programs for Alcohol and
   Drug Problems
2575 Bittern Street, NE
Salem, OR 97310
(503) 378-2163

PENNSYLVANIA
Department of Health
Office of Drug and Alcohol
   Programs
Commonwealth and Forster Avenues
Health and Welfare Building
P.O. Box 90
Harrisburg, PA 17108
(717) 787-9857

RHODE ISLAND
Department of Mental Health,
   Mental Retardation and Hospitals
Division of Substance Abuse
Substance Abuse Administration
   Building
Cranston, RI 02920
(401) 464-2091

SOUTH CAROLINA
Commission on Alcohol and Drug
   Abuse
3700 Forest Drive
Columbia, SC 29204
(803) 758-2521

SOUTH DAKOTA
Department of Health
Division of Alcohol and Drug Abuse
523 East Capitol, Joe Foss Building
Pierre, SD 57501
(605) 773-4806

TENNESSEE
Department of Mental Health and
   Mental Retardation
Alcohol and Drug Abuse Services
505 Deaderick Street
James K. Polk Building, Fourth Floor
Nashville, TN 37219
(615) 741-1921

TEXAS
Commission on Alcoholism
809 Sam Houston State Office Building
Austin, TX 78701
(512) 475-2577

Department of Community Affairs
Drug Abuse Prevention Division
2015 South Interstate Highway 35
P.O. Box 13166
Austin, TX 78711
(512) 443-4100

UTAH
Department of Social Services
Division of Alcoholism and Drugs
150 West North Temple
Suite 350
P.O. Box 2500
Salt Lake City, UT 84110
(801) 533-6532

VERMONT
Agency of Human Services
Department of Social and
   Rehabilitation Services
Alcohol and Drug Abuse Division
103 South Main Street
Waterbury, VT 05676
(802) 241-2170

VIRGINIA
Department of Mental Health and
   Mental Retardation
Division of Substance Abuse
109 Governor Street
P.O. Box 1797
Richmond, VA 23214
(804) 786-5313

WASHINGTON
Department of Social and Health
   Service
Bureau of Alcohol and Substance
   Abuse
Office Building—44 W
Olympia, WA 98504
(206) 753-5866

WEST VIRGINIA
Department of Health
Office of Behavioral Health Services
Division on Alcoholism and Drug
   Abuse
1800 Washington Street East
Building 3 Room 451
Charleston, WV 25305
(304) 348-2276

WISCONSIN
Department of Health and Social
   Services
Division of Community Services
Bureau of Community Programs
Alcohol and Other Drug Abuse
   Program Office
1 West Wilson Street
P.O. Box 7851
Madison, WI 53707
(608) 266-2717

WYOMING
Alcohol and Drug Abuse Programs
Hathaway Building
Cheyenne, WY 82002
(307) 777-7115, Ext. 7118

GUAM
Mental Health & Substance Abuse
   Agency
P.O. Box 20999
Guam 96921

PUERTO RICO
Department of Addiction Control
   Services
Alcohol Abuse Programs
P.O. Box B-Y Rio Piedras Station
Rio Piedras, PR 00928
(809) 763-5014

Department of Addiction Control
   Services
Drug Abuse Programs
P.O. Box B-Y Rio Piedras Station
Rio Piedras, PR 00928
(809) 764-8140

VIRGIN ISLANDS
Division of Mental Health,
   Alcoholism & Drug Dependency
   Services
P.O. Box 7329
Saint Thomas, Virgin Islands 00801
(809) 774-7265

AMERICAN SAMOA
LBJ Tropical Medical Center
Department of Mental Health Clinic
Pago Pago, American Samoa 96799

TRUST TERRITORIES
Director of Health Services
Office of the High Commissioner
Saipan, Trust Territories 96950

Further Reading

Ayd, F.J., Jr., and Blackwell, B. *Discoveries in Biological Psychiatry*. Philadelphia/Toronto: J.B. Lippincott Company, 1970.

Caldwell, A.E. *Origins of Psychopharmacology from CPZ to LSD*. Springfield: Charles C. Thomas, 1970.

Diagnostic and Statistical Manual of Mental Disorders (DSM III), 3rd edition. Washington, D.C.: American Psychiatric Association, 1980.

Gilman, A.G., Goodman, L.S., and Gilman, A. *The Pharmacological Basis of Therapeutics*, 6th edition. New York: Macmillan Publishing Co., Inc., 1980.

Klein, D.F., Gittelman, R., Quitkin, F., and Rifkin, A. *Diagnosis and Drug Treatment of Psychiatric Disorders: Adults and Children*, 2nd edition. Baltimore: Williams & Wilkins, 1980.

Lickey, M.E. *Drugs for Mental Illness: A Revolution in Psychiatry*. New York/San Francisco: W.H. Freeman and Company, 1983.

Sheehan, S. *Is There No Place on Earth for Me?* Boston: Houghton Mifflin, 1982.

Swazey, J.P. *Chlorpromazine in Psychiatry: A Study of Therapeutic Innovation*. Cambridge, Massachusetts: MIT Press, 1974.

Glossary

addiction a condition caused by repeated drug use, characterized by a compulsive urge to continue using the drug, a tendency to increase the dosage, and physiological and/or psychological dependence

affective disorder a disorder that alters the expression of an individual's mood state

akathisia a condition sometimes produced by antipsychotic drugs and characterized by restlessness and an inability to sit down because the thought of doing so produces extreme anxiety

anesthetic a drug that produces loss of sensation, sometimes with loss of consciousness

antidepressant drug a drug that acts to relieve the symptoms of depression

antihistamine a drug that inhibits the action of histamine and thus reduces the allergic response

antipsychotic drug a drug, such as chlorpromazine, that calms a person who is in a psychotic state

axon the part of the neuron along which the nerve impulse travels away from the cell body

barbiturate a drug that causes depression of the central nervous system, generally used to reduce anxiety

benzodiazepine antianxiety and sedative drugs such as Valium

chlorpromazine a tranquilizing drug, such as Thorazine, used in the treatment of psychotic states

cocaine the primary psychoactive ingredient in the coca plant; used as a behavioral stimulant

delusion a false belief that is not based on external stimulation and that is inconsistent with the individual's knowledge and personal experiences

dendrite the hairlike structure that protrudes from and carries signals toward the neural cell body, and on which receptor sites are located

depression a sometimes overwhelming emotional state characterized by feelings of inadequacy and hopelessness, accompanied by a decrease in physical and psychological activity

dopamine a neurotransmitter produced by the adrenal

gland; it has a marked effect on body temperature and metabolic rate and on the nervous system and cardio-vascular system

dopamine-blocking drug a drug that interferes with the transmission of nerve impulses in the body by blocking the action of dopamine in the body

electroshock therapy a technique sometimes effective in treating agitated psychosis, characterized by the use of an electric current to stimulate the brain and induce involuntary muscle contractions

enzyme an organic compound that induces chemical changes in other substances without being changed itself

galactorrhea the extreme flow of milk from the female breast, sometimes caused by chlorpromazine

goiter an enlargement of the thyroid gland, producing symptoms such as bulging eyeballs, tremors of the fingers and hands, and an increase in metabolic rate

hallucination a sensory impression that has no basis in reality

hashish a psychoactive substance made from the resin and the dried and pressed flowers and leaves of the marijuana plant

hypnotic a drug that induces sleep or dulls the senses

hypotension a decrease in blood pressure

hypothyroidism a decrease in thyroid secretion that causes a lowered metabolic rate, and such symptoms as obesity, low blood pressure and pulse, and depressed muscular activity

lithium a chemical element that occurs in nature as a white metal and is used to prevent recurrent manic episodes and to treat manic-depressive psychosis

lobotomy a type of brain surgery that severs communication between specific parts of the brain and is sometimes used to relieve some forms of mental illness

LSD lysergic acid diethylamide; a hallucinogen derived from a fungus that grows on rye or from morning-glory seeds

manic characterized by excitement and mental and physical hyperactivity

manic-depressive psychosis a mental disorder characterized by abrupt alternations of depression and mania

metabolism the chemical changes in the living cell by

which energy is provided for the vital processes and activities and by which new material is assimilated to repair cell structures; or, the process that uses enzymes to convert one substance into compounds that can be easily eliminated from the body

mood-stabilizing drug a drug that reduces or eliminates fluctuations in mood

mood state a prolonged emotion that affects one's entire emotional life

neuroleptic a drug that produces symptoms that resemble the symptoms of diseases of the nervous system

neuron a cell that conducts electrochemical signals

neurotic related to a disorder of the thought processes that is not characterized by a loss of contact with reality and not due to a disease of the nervous system; symptoms include fatigue, anxiety, compulsiveness, and hypochondria

neurotransmitter a chemical that travels from the axon of one neuron, across the synaptic gap, and to the receptor site on the dendrite of an adjacent neuron, thus allowing communication between neural cells

organic brain syndrome a large group of mental disorders resulting from brain damage due to physical illness or trauma

paranoia a mental condition characterized by suspiciousness, fear, delusions, and, in extreme cases, hallucinations

parasympathetic nervous system the part of the central nervous system that controls involuntary bodily activity such as sweating and contraction of the intestine

Parkinson's disease a chronic nervous disease that creates a lack of dopamine in certain brain cells; it produces symptoms such as fine tremors, facial expressionlessness, and muscle weakness and rigidity; its cause is unknown, though it mainly affects older people

PCP phencyclidine; a drug first used as an anesthetic but later discontinued because of its severe adverse side effects; today abused for its stimulant, depressant, and/or hallucinogenic effects

periodic catatonia a rare syndrome of repeated episodes of rigidity and loss of speech

phenothiazine the parent chemical from which a certain

class of tranquilizers that include chlorpromazine is synthesized

placebo effect   a pharmacologic effect on a symptom produced by a substance that is either pharmacologically inert (produces no effects on the body) or is active only in the treatment of unrelated symptoms

prolactin   a hormone that stimulates milk production in nursing mothers

psychiatrist   a medical doctor who has continued his or her education to study mental disease and who is trained to distinguish between the symptoms of physical disease or neurological illness and psychological disease; he or she can prescribe drugs

psychoanalysis   a form of psychotherapy that grew out of Austrian neurologist Sigmund Freud's (1856–1939) observations of neurotics; based on the theory that mental illness is caused by the repression of painful or undesirable past experiences and that by bringing forgotten memories to the surface, the source of psychological conflicts can be located; proponents believe that the patient's awareness of the conflicts reduces or eliminates psychological disorders

psychologist   a person who usually has an advanced degree, often a Ph.D., in clinical psychology and who practices one or more of the many types of psychotherapy

psychopharmacology   the study of the effects of drugs on the mind

psychosis   abnormal or pathological behavior that includes the loss of touch with reality, and occasionally hallucinations and delusions

psychosurgery   surgical intervention into the brain to treat neurological disorders

psychotherapeutic   a drug that is used in the treatment of psychological disorders

psychotherapist   an individual trained to use one of the many forms of therapy that evolved from the study of human behavior and the psychological theories that developed; psychotherapists treat disorders not with drugs but through techniques such as suggestions, reeducation, hypnotism, and psychoanalysis

reserpine   a drug with tranquilizing effects that is extracted from the root of *Rauwolfia serpentina*, a plant native to India, and used in the treatment of psychosis

schizophrenia   a chronic disorder characterized by a loss of touch with reality and symptoms such as paranoia, delusions, and hallucinations

sedative   a drug that produces a soothing or tranquilizing effect

sympathetic nervous system   a system of nerves within the central nervous system that, during an emergency, elicits responses of alertness, excitement, and alarm and controls the expenditure of necessary energy

synaptic gap   the gap between the axon and dendrite of two adjacent neurons across which neurotransmitters travel

tardive dyskinesia   a neurological effect of antipsychotic-drug use that occurs late in treatment and is characterized by involuntary mouth movements, and in severe cases, slow, rhythmic, automatic arm and torso movements

thyroid gland   a gland located in the neck that produces a hormone that affects growth, development, and metabolic rate

tolerance   a decrease of susceptibility to the effects of a drug due to its continued administration, resulting in the user's need to increase the drug dosage in order to achieve the effects experienced previously

tranquilizer   a drug that has calming, relaxing effects

tricyclic antidepressants   a class of drugs whose members have three rings of carbon atoms in each molecule, and that is used therapeutically to relieve depression and elevate mood in individuals who are psychologically depressed

urate   a chemical normally found in the urine

Index

affective disorder, 53
see also depression
akathisia, 45
see also chlorpromazine; drugs, side effects
alcohol, 25, 31
see also drugs
alpha adrenergic blocking agents, 40
see also chlorpromazine
amines, 56, 60, 69, 73
see also dopamine; neurotransmitter
amino acids, 60
amphetamines, 25
see also drugs
angel dust see phencyclidine
anxiety, 25
see also depression; mental illness
aspirin, 31–32
see also drugs
atropine, 40–41
see also chlorpromazine; drugs
barbiturates, 48
see also drugs
behavior therapy, 21
see also mental illness, treatment
benzodiazepines, 48
see also drugs
Cade, John, 23, 66–67
see also lithium; manic-depressive psychosis; mental illness, treatment
caffeine, 25
see also drugs
Cannabis sativa, 21
see also drugs; marijuana
carbamazepine (Tegretol), 71
see also lithium; manic-depressive psychosis; mental illness; treatment
Chloramead see chlorpromazine
2-chlorphenothiazine, 26
see also chlorpromazine
chlorpromazine, 22–23, 26–27, 37–43, 59, 68
see also drugs, antipsychotic; mental illness, treatment; schizophrenia
cocaine, 25
see also drugs
Controlled Substances Act of 1970, 25
see also drugs, legal status

depression, 23, 25–26, 53–63, 65
see also drugs, antidepressant; mental illness
detoxification, 31
diazepam see Valium
dopamine, 28, 37, 42, 44
see also chlorpromazine; drugs, antipsychotic; drugs, mechanism of action; schizophrenia
drugs
antianxiety, 25, 48
antidepressant, 27, 56–62, 70
antihistaminic, 25, 28, 59
antipsychotic, 27, 37–50, 70
classification, 24–26
dopamine-blocking, 28, 37, 41
dose-effect relationship, 30–31, 48, 50
duration of action, 31
interactions with other drugs, 41, 60–62
legal status, 25
mechanism of action, 41, 56–57, 69–70
metabolism, 38
mood-stabilizing, 27, 70
names, 26–29
neuroleptic, 27
over-the-counter (OTC), 24–25
prescription, 25
psychotherapeutic, 22–29, 31–32, 35
schedules, 25
self-administered, 25–26
side effects, 25–26, 30–32, 38–48, 59–62, 69–71
structural effects, 30, 37, 73
see also mental illness, treatment
electroshock therapy see depression; mental illness, treatment
enzyme, 60
see also monoamine oxidase inhibitors
"euphoric quietude," 22
FDA see Food and Drug Administration
fluphenazine (Prolixin), 41
see also drugs, antipsychotic
Food and Drug Administration (FDA), 25
4560 RP see chlorpromazine
Freud, Sigmund, 21
see also mental illness, treatment,

history
galactorrhea, 42
  see also drugs, side effects
generic names, 26
goiter, 69
  see also drugs, side effects
group names, 27–28
Haldol see haloperidol
hallucinations, 34, 41, 47
  see also mental illness, symptoms
haloperidol (Haldol), 43
  see also drugs, antipsychotic
hashish, 21
  see also drugs
Hashish and Mental Illness, 21
heroin, 25
  see also drugs
histamine, 22
  see also drugs, antihistaminic
Hofmann, Albert, 22
hypotension, postural, 59
  see also drugs, side effects
hypothyroidism, 69–70
  see also drugs, side effects
imipramine, 56, 59
  see also drugs, antidepressant;
    tricyclic antidepressants
iproniazid, 56
  see also drugs, antidepressant;
    monoamine oxidase inhibitors
Kuhn, Roland, 56
  see also mental illness, treatment;
    tricyclic antidepressants
Laborit, Henri, 22
  see also mental illness, treatment,
    history
Largactil see chlorpromazine
L-DOPA, 44
  see also dopamine; Parkinson's
    disease
lithium, 23, 50, 67–71
  carbonate, 68
  urate, 67
  see also drugs, antipsychotic; manic-
    depressive psychosis; mental
    illness, treatment
LSD see lysergic acid diethylamide
lysergic acid diethylamide (LSD), 22
  see also drugs
Magnetic Resonance Imaging, 73

  see also mental illness, diagnosis
mania, 23, 47–48, 65–66
  see also mental illness, symptoms
manic-depressive psychosis, 23, 50,
    65–71
  see also mental illness
marijuana, 25, 33
  see also drugs
Medical Journal of Australia, 68
  see also mental illness, treatment,
    history
Mellaril see thioridazine
mental illness
  case studies, 32–35, 54–55, 65
  diagnosis, 33–35
  epidemiology, 37–38
  physiologic basis, 19, 21–22, 32, 34,
    37, 56–57, 70
  symptoms, 32–33, 38, 54–55, 65–66
  theories of, 19, 21–22, 50
  treatment
    drugs and, 19, 22–24, 35, 38–39,
      47–51, 56–62, 66–71, 73
    electroshock therapy, 51, 62, 68
    history, 21–24, 56, 66–68
    hospitalization, 38, 63
    megavitamin, 50–51
    professionals involved in, 19–21
    psychotherapy, 20–21, 32, 35, 49,
      51, 63
    surgical, 51
    see also depression; drugs; manic-
      depressive psychosis;
      schizophrenia
monoamine oxidase, 60
monoamine oxidase inhibitors, 56, 60–62
  see also depression; mental illness,
    treatment
mood state, 53
  see also depression
Moreau de Tours, J. J., 21
  see also mental illness, treatment,
    history
Nardil see phenelzine
nervous system
  parasympathetic, 40–41
  sympathetic, 40
  see also dopamine; drugs, side
    effects; neurotransmitter
neurosurgeon, 22

neurotransmitter, 28, 37, 56
 see also amines; dopamine; drugs,
  mechanism of action; mental
  illness, physiologic basis
nicotine, 25
 see also drugs
organic brain syndrome, 39
 see also mental illness
OTCs see drugs, over-the-counter
paranoia, 33
 see also mental illness, symptoms
parasympathetic nervous system
 see nervous system
Parkinson's disease, 43–44
 see also drugs, side effects
Parkinson's mask, 44
 see also drugs, side effects
PCP see phencyclidine
periodic catatonia, 70
 see also lithium
PET scanning, 73
 see also mental illness, diagnosis
phencyclidine (angel dust; PCP), 41
 see also drugs
phenelzine (Nardil), 60–61
 see also drugs, antidepressant; mental
  illness, treatment; monoamine
  oxidase inhibitors
phenothiazine, 28, 37, 56
 see also chlorpromazine; drugs,
  antipsychotic
photosensitivity, 42
 see also drugs, side effects
placebo, 51
postural hypotension see hypotension,
  postural
prolactin inhibiting factor, 42
 see also dopamine; drugs, side effects
Prolixin see fluphenazine
Promapar see chlorpromazine
promethazine, 22
 see also chlorpromazine; drugs,
  antipsychotic
psychiatrist, 20, 34–35, 55, 65
 see also mental illness, treatment
psychoanalysis, 21
 see also mental illness, treatment
psychoanalyst, 21
 see also mental illness, treatment
psychologist, 21

 see also mental illness, treatment
psychopharmacology, 22, 29
 see also drugs; mental illness,
  treatment
psychosis, 34–35, 37–38
 see also mental illness
psychosurgery see mental illness,
  treatment
psychotherapist, 20
 see also mental illness, treatment
psychotherapy see mental illness,
  treatment
Rauwolfia serpentina (snakeroot), 24, 56
repression, 21
 see also mental illness, treatment
reserpine, 24, 56
 see also drugs, antipsychotic; mental
  illness, treatment
schizophrenia, 35, 37–39
 see also mental illness
snakeroot see Rauwolfia serpentina
suicide, 53–55, 59, 63
 see also depression
sympathetic nervous system
 see nervous system
"talking therapy," 20
 see also mental illness, treatment
tardive dyskinesia, 45–47, 49–50
 see also drugs, side effects
Tegretol see carbamazepine
thioridazine (Mellaril), 39, 43
 see also chlorpromazine; drugs,
  antipsychotic; mental illness,
  treatment
Thorazine see chlorpromazine
trade names, 27
tranquilizer, 24
 see also drugs
tricyclic antidepressants, 28–29, 56,
  58–61
 see also depression; mental illness,
  treatment; monoamine oxidase
  inhibitors
tyramine, 60
 see also drugs, side effects;
  monoamine oxidase inhibitors
urates, 67
 see also lithium
Valium (diazepam), 48
 see also drugs

Robert Byck, M.D., is a professor of psychiatry and pharmacology at Yale University School of Medicine and a practicing clinical psychiatrist and pharmacologist. He was the editor of Freud's *Cocaine Papers.*

Solomon H. Snyder, M.D., is Distinguished Service Professor of Neuroscience, Pharmacology and Psychiatry at The Johns Hopkins University School of Medicine. He has served as president of the Society for Neuroscience and in 1978 received the Albert Lasker Award in Medical Research. He has authored *Uses of Marijuana, Madness and the Brain, The Troubled Mind, Biological Aspects of Mental Disorder,* and edited *Perspective in Neuropharmacology: A Tribute to Julius Axelrod.* Professor Snyder was a research associate with Dr. Axelrod at the National Institutes of Health.

Barry L. Jacobs, Ph.D., is currently a professor in the program of neuroscience at Princeton University. Professor Jacobs is author of *Serotonin Neurotransmission and Behavior* and *Hallucinogens: Neurochemical, Behavioral and Clinical Perspectives.* He has written many journal articles in the field of neuroscience and contributed numerous chapters to books on behavior and brain science. He has been a member of several panels of the National Institute of Mental Health.

Jerome H. Jaffe, M.D., formerly professor of psychiatry at the College of Physicians and Surgeons, Columbia University, has been named recently Director of the Addiction Research Center of the National Institute on Drug Abuse. Dr. Jaffe is also a psychopharmacologist and has conducted research on a wide range of addictive drugs and developed treatment programs for addicts. He has acted as Special Consultant to the President on Narcotics and Dangerous Drugs and was the first director of the White House Special Action Office for Drug Abuse Prevention.